HOLLYWOOD HOUSES

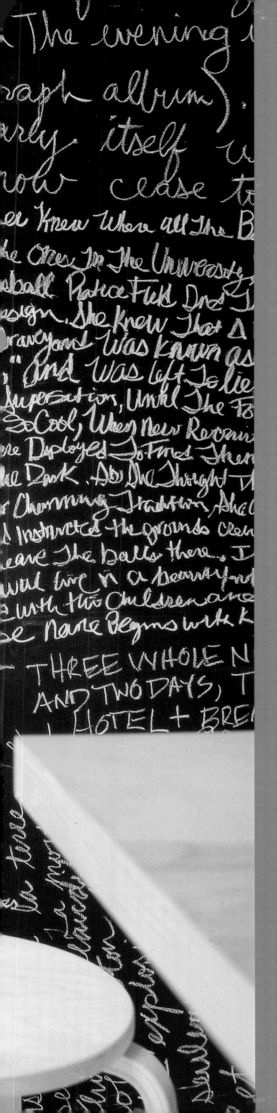

HOLLYWOOD HOUSES

BY TIM STREET-PORTER AND
DIANE DORRANS SAEKS

With 183 illustrations, 181 in colour

Thames & Hudson

First published in the United Kingdom in 2004 by
Thames & Hudson Ltd, 181A High Holborn, London WC1V 7QX

www.thamesandhudson.com

Originally published as *Hollywood Style* in the United States of America
in 2004 by Rizzoli International Publications, Inc,. New York.

Text © 2004 Diane Dorrans Saeks
Principle photography © 2004 Tim Street-Porter

British Library Cataloguing-in-Publication Data
A catalogue record for this book is available from the British Library

ISBN 0-500-54295-3

Designed by Subtitle

Printed and bound in China

HOLLYWOOD HOUSES

BY TIM STREET-PORTER AND DIANE DORRANS SAEKS

TABLE OF CONTENTS

A LAUTNER MASTERPIECE
With its view of the HOLLYWOOD sign on the hillside in the distance, this 1949 Los Feliz house by John Lautner is currently the residence of actress Kelly Lynch and screenwriter Mitch Glazer. When they acquired it—this is their second Lautner restoration—it had fallen into disrepair. Recent extensive restoration of the house was directed by architect Helena Arahuete who worked closely with John Lautner for twenty years and had access to all original drawings, records and files.

INTRODUCTION
THE ROAD TO WONDERFUL
BY DIANE DORRANS SAEKS

"The real voyage of discovery consists not in seeking new landscapes, but in having new eyes," said Marcel Proust, who knew a thing or three about savoring the moment and the sensual recollection of joyful times. Proust was immured in Paris, of course, but his optimistic and insightful suggestion could wisely be applied to considerations of California and, in particular, to Los Angeles and its architecture and interior design.

Beginner's mind. Beginner's eyes. That is the way to approach and discover Los Angeles and Hollywood, detouring past the cliches to discover the pure beauty, the delights, the fantasies, the wit, the hilarity, and the pleasure of lives well lived in splendid houses and luscious landscapes in year-round springtime.

Each curve of the road—Rodeo Drive, Lookout Mountain Drive, Bellagio Road, Sunset Boulevard, Benedict Canyon, the wilds of Los Feliz—brings forth the architecture of self-expression and self-realization beneath the palm trees.

Just as movie-makers can recreate John Lautner's iconic Chemosphere house on a sound stage, and a hotel designer will rebuild the chateau of Chenonceaux as the Chateau Marmont on Sunset Boulevard, so a homeowner with a dream can perch a Tudor mansion on a Hollywood precipice, or rebuild Persepolis or Versailles in a tangle of rampaging tropical greenery in Beverly Hills.

A DIZZY DAY OF ARCHITECTURE Walking into the living room of the house architect Rudoph Schindler built for himself on Kings Road in 1921, a visitor is transported to his optimistic moment when all architectural ideas and missions seemed possible. There, on a leafy lot in West Hollywood, Schindler built a rooftop "sleeping basket" for healthy outdoor repose, and doors that slide and disappear to elide the borders between lawn and living room.

Los Angeles architecture can be subtle, sleek, and intellectual or decorative, romantic, and wistful of an earlier, more genteel era.

The hills of Silver Lake, the Grande Corniche–like switchbacks of Whitley Heights and the flatlands of Beverly Hills offer a feast for lovers of design traditions, experimental architecture, and smoke-and-mirrors cinematic dreams.

In one dizzy day some of the world's most admired and influential architecture can be appraised. A swoop downtown offers the superbly choreographed steel abstractions of Frank O. Gehry at the glamorous new Walt Disney Concert Hall, while a quick loop over to Hollywood yields the pure poetry of the revived Pantages Theatre, gloriously gilded and grand, the setting for the Academy Awards until the fifties.

Architecture of the twenties, thirties, and forties is gaining new respect. Architect Craig Ellwood's functional aesthetic bungalows at the Chateau Marmont are in demand by those who appreciate their transparent walls and gracefully expressed modernist ideals. Sheltered beneath old elms, his retreats are cool, calm, and elegantly simple.

Perhaps to counter the reputation of Los Angeles as a tear-down city with no appreciation of the past, style-conscious denizens are buying up neglected landmark houses and bringing them back to life.

Los Angeles vintage design guru Cameron Silver

found a neglected Rudolph Schindler house on a hillside in Silver Lake, and commissioned Leo Marmol and Ron Radziner, the leading renovation and historical restoration architects, to rethink the house and erase misdirected sixties additions.

"To live in a Schindler house is a constant pleasure because we are moment by moment aware of the mind and intellect of this great architect," said Silver. "The house is living history. I like to keep Sundays free so that I can just hang out at home, relax on the terrace, and enjoy the house."

A LOVE OF HISTORY "There's a misconception that there's no design history in Los Angeles and that everything is imported and fake," said interior designer Michael Smith, who deftly designs low-key interiors for clients like Cindy Crawford, Dustin Hoffman, Richard Gere, and Michelle Pfeiffer.

"There have been beautiful houses and fine, polished interiors here for more than a hundred years," said Smith, who recently completed the interiors of a house that was designed in the early thirties by architect James Dolena. One of the first decorators of the house was T. H. Robsjohn-Gibbings, today a design icon. The house had great bones, said Smith, who gave the rooms contemporary polish and elegance with Chippendale armchairs, an eighteenth-century Swedish chandelier, and dramatic curtains of billowing lemon and yellow silk.

"We had Spanish Colonial houses on vast open tracts, and later grand mansions downtown early in the last century," said Smith. "Many would say that Hollywood residents reinvent life every five minutes and are recklessly unaware of context or appropriateness. In my experience, people here are very design-aware and style-savvy. Los Angeles has inspired the world. Film sets and movie interiors have influenced the realms of design for more than eighty years."

Far from forgetting their design and architecture legacy, decorators and architects reference it constantly and with great reverence.

Designer Kelly Wearstler looked to actor/interior designer Billy Haines for the curvy armchairs and Hollywood Regency interiors of the Viceroy hotel in Santa Monica, and Maison 140 in Beverly Hills.

In Holmby Hills, architects Brian Tichenor and Raun Thorp revived a house designed in 1940 by modernist architect Harwell Hamilton Harris, who was a follower of Frank Lloyd Wright, and a student of Schindler. The architect was in partnership for a time with Neutra. Their house shows the influences of Wright, traditional Japanese architecture, as well as Neutra.

"We characterize it as having a Frank Lloyd Wright roof and plan with a Case Study body," said Thorp.

There is no one Hollywood Style, no single Los Angeles look, no interior design that everyone aspires to. Rather, this is the land of individualists, dreamers, real-estate mad people who lust to make their imprint.

At the same moment architect Richard Neutra was paring down his logically managed environments, and stripping down the friperries of the past, designers like Billy Haines and Tony Duquette, a set designer, were embellishing their décor to give indifferent architecture the grandeur to which it aspired.

MOVIE MAGIC
Previous page With its bold curves and glittering valley view, this architectural interior looks like the legendary Chemosphere house or one of John Lautner's other classics. In fact, it's an artful and very convincing movie set created as the sexy residence for the villain of the first "Charlie's Angels" movie, starring Cameron Diaz, Lucy Liu and Drew Barrymore. Production designers got permission from the John Lautner Foundation for their homage. See the real thing on pages 5, 13.

DREAM COLONY In a leafy ravine high above Beverly Hills, decorator/artist Tony Duquette built Dawnridge, his psychedelic confection of seventeenth-century landscapes, gilded dolphins, silvery Thai Buddhas, Mogul embroidery, Venetian crystal baubles, scallop-shell decorated chandeliers, ferns, orchids, and star cast-offs that has been the fetishy setting for sexed-up Gucci ads and a slew of *Vogue* editorial pages. The glamour of Dawnridge was magical.

Award-winning costume designer Theadora van Runkle recalls arriving for a party there straight from a movie set in Rome.

"I'd been on location with Marcello Mastroianni and Vittorio de Sica for six months, and as we arrived at Dawnridge, the rooms blazed with ten thousand candles," said van Runkle. "Tony's rooms were like the jewel casket of a potentate—luxurious and out-of-this-world. The glitterati arrived, flash-bulbs popped, and it was everything one imagines a Hollywood party to be."

Glamour was everything.

Hollywood insider Denise Hale recalls landing in Los Angeles from New York in 1961, after marrying director Vincente Minelli on New Year's Eve 1960 at the Palm Springs house of Kirk Douglas.

"Billy Haines had a complete monopoly on decorating at that time," Hale recalled. "The houses he designed were so beautiful, and only the In group—the greatest actors, the top directors, the international crowd, the old guard—saw them."

Hale, a fixture at the *Vanity Fair* Oscar party, recalled arriving at Jack and Ann Warner's on Angelo Drive in Beverly Hills house for a grand gala.

"There was a beautiful long driveway, and at the front door to greet guests was a butler in tails," said Hale. "The rooms were full of great art, European decor, the finest antiques. I'd seen rooms like that in Europe but never in Los Angeles. It was top, top, top. The tails are gone forever, but interiors are still elegant. But they're less formal."

Designers and architects note that Los Angeles is no longer a playground for hedonists and black-tie dinner parties are few and far between.

"Everyone is working so hard and then they go home to sleep," said architect Raun Thorp. "It's a company town, is the refrain, and everyone is focused on their work. Thank goodness they want wonderful houses to go home to. Our clients like to have beautiful surroundings to reassure them of their successes, and the reasons why they work so hard. Life here can be very beautiful indeed.

PARALLEL UNIVERSE The clean, abstract compositions and forward-thinking philosophy of progressive architecture exist as an almost parallel universe to the tradition-loving interior design and antiques world of Los Angeles.

Sleek glass and steel and concrete houses have been emblems for this West Coast utopia since Frank Lloyd Wright, R. M. Schindler, and Richard Neutra arrived in Los Angeles in the twenties and thirties, drawn by the new-world promise of Los Angeles, its lush natural setting, friendly climate, vast open tracts, and new money.

Schindler and Neutra, perhaps the most referenced

architects in Los Angeles, applied their intellectual rigor and religious fervor for healthy living close to nature (think Schindler's rooftop "sleeping baskets" and Neutra's elegant glass pavilions with almost transparent walls).

Architects and industrial designers Ray and Charles Eames, Pierre Koenig, Craig Ellwood, and Raphael Soriano pushed these pioneer concepts further with their Case Study houses, and made Southern California one of the liveliest and most influential laboratories of twentieth-century architecture.

Enclaves of Modernist landmarks cling to the hillsides in Silver Lake, Santa Monica Canyon, West Hollywood, Los Feliz, and Santa Monica, where Cedric Gibbons, Ray Kappe, Richard Neutra and new-generation architects like Patrick Tighe. Lorcan O'Herlihy, Barton Myers are making their marks today.

Give an architect like John Lautner an impossibly steep handkerchief-sized plot and a few tons of concrete and in 1960 he will invent the mushroom-shaped Chemosphere house which projects up and out from its perch. It will be celebrated as one of the architectural icons of the twentieth-century and then "blown up" in a *Lethal Weapon* series film, before inspiring the ultimate villain pad in a *Charlie's Angels* movie. Hollywood takes its architecture very seriously.

Offer Richard Neutra a few hillside acres overlooking a reservoir, and he will sketch shrines to the promise of healthy California living. Bring R. M. Schindler to California and he'll make walls as light as those in a Shinto shrine, and pay homage to the garden with doors and windows that gaze at velvety lawns and sun-washed lily ponds.

Rigorous architecture, clearly, has its moment of romantic hedonism in Los Angeles. And the willy-nilly whims for Louis xv–inspired mansions, space-age beach houses and Palladian palaces can be seen as a joyous celebration of personal expression, carefree wonder, and a belief in seizing a moment of glory.

Everything under the sun can be built in Los Angeles. Dreams are fulfilled every day. And everything is possible in this best of all possible worlds.

Los Angeles is the most seductive of settings. The voices that roared that there is no culture have been stilled. Richard Meier's Getty Center, Frank Gehry's new Disney Concert Hall, performances by the Los Angeles Philharmonic, and exhibitions at numerous galleries and world-class museums confer stature and richness to the city and its surroundings.

Art aside, Los Angeles is till the ultimate playground. Even an ordinary afternoon in Los Angeles has a sunstruck sense of magical reality. A swoop along Melrose to Maxfield to check out vintage Hermès luggage, a sweep down Wilshire to Barney's New York to admire Gem Palace jewels, or an hour checking the Manolo Blahniks at Neiman Marcus or antiques along La Cienega make life seem luscious. A few quiet moments with Frank L. Baum volumes at the Heritage Book Shop on Melrose, lunch at Bastide, a dive into Book Soup, a Negroni at the Bel-Air bar, and the day is even sweeter. Even Voltaire, that most astute observer, would smile.

ROMANTIC OVERTURE
For his own house, interior
designer Martyn Lawrence-
Bullard pulled out all the
stops with zebra-striped Louis
XVI-style chairs, a dramatic
mezzotint, a scrolled console
table, and marble fragments.
Some of the pieces date back
to his boyhood in London.
"Everything you love will
work together, and creates, in
effect, a kind of self-portrait,"
said the designer.

CHAPTER 1
CLASSIC HOLLYWOOD

A DELICIOUS AIR OF MYSTERY HANGS OVER HOUSES IN THE HOLLYWOOD HILLS AND ALONG THE PALMY AVENUES OF BEVERLY HILLS AND WEST HOLLYWOOD. SOME INTERIORS HINT AT CEDRIC GIBBONS, WHILE OTHERS WERE ENRICHED BY WORLD TRAVEL, MOVIE-STAR BUDGETS, AND A HOST OF FINE CRAFTSMEN WHO DEVOTED THEIR LIVES AND CREATIVITY TO MAKE THESE DOMESTIC DREAMS A REALITY.

Hidden above curvy streets that reach heavenward and swathed in tall hedges and lush landscapes, moguls' mansions and pop palazzi and their surroundings seem as superbly art-directed and unreal as a movie set.

Designers and architects have seized every opportunity to fulfill life-long fantasies for their clients. A Grand Tour to Tuscany and Rome, visions of Versailles, a trek through maharajas' palaces in Jaipur, or over-heated voyages around Angkor Wat could all inspire an estate, a chateau, ballrooms, a baroque stairway, or a pavilion in a canyon.

Tony Duquette, an artist and set designer, would not let reality intrude on his imagination. And he never saw a surface that could not be embellished and enriched and then collaged and gilded. Dawnridge, one of his many residences, transcends time and is now prized as a decadent setting for fashion shoots.

Was it the balmy weather of Southern California that incited Frank Lloyd Wright to create some of his finest work, or was it his clients' dreams, altruism and funds? In Pasadena, Wright sculpted concrete blocks into poetry and left a legacy of buildings that are revered around the world.

SUNLIGHT AND SHADOW

ONE OF FRANK LLOYD WRIGHT'S GRANDEST ACHIEVEMENTS, A ROMANTIC CONCRETE-BLOCK VILLA IN PASADENA, MAKES A GRACEFUL REVIVAL

"Architecture is the triumph of human imagination over materials, methods, and men," said Frank Lloyd Wright at his most philosophical. "Architecture is at least the geometric pattern of things, of life, of the human and social world. It is at best that magic framework of reality that we sometimes touch upon when we use the word 'order'."

Wright's words, written in 1930, are most apt for a small villa he built in 1923 in Pasadena for Alice Millard, an antiquarian book dealer. It was the first concrete textile-block construction house in the United States.

Millard, whose brief for Wright was an Italian villa for indoor/outdoor living, dubbed the house La Miniatura. It is superbly situated near Brookside Park and within walking distance of both the Gamble House by Greene and Greene, and the Rose Bowl. The villa, which was originally planned as a winter retreat for the Chicago-based Millard, was the first of four textile-block houses constructed by Wright in the Los Angeles area.

"What about the concrete block?" asked Wright. "It was the cheapest (and ugliest) thing in the building world. It lived mostly in the architectural gutter as an imitation of rock-faced stone. Why not see what could be done with that gutter rat? And with the whole brought into some broad, practical scheme of general treatment, why would it not be fit for a new phase of our modern architecture? It might be permanent, noble, beautiful."

The relief patterns of the concrete blocks which were custom-crafted for La Miniatura are deftly arranged to give the exterior of the house a subtle rhythm, a textural silhouette, and a sense of rising out of the earth.

La Miniatura's two-story high living room is delicately lit by pierced, patterned blocks and overlooks a reflecting pool surrounded by gardens. The house straddles an arroyo, a rush of runoff water in winter and completely parched in summer, and the dramatic Pasadena siting appears to be a precursor or Fallingwater in its thrust over water.

"Many people think that the house looks like a Mayan temple," noted Annie Kelly, a Los Angeles designer who specializes in historical restoration. "In the elegant original drawings, which I consulted, the house looks like both a Mayan temple and rather Japanese in style. Wright was working on the Imperial Hotel in Tokyo at the time, and the influences are there."

Kelly recently worked with architect Michael Mekeel on restoration and preservation for La Miniatura.

"The house had fallen into disrepair, but its craftsman detailing and small rooms were largely intact," said Kelly.

The finished house was not at all Italian in feeling, as Alice Millard had hoped, so she completed the furnishings with a Mediterranean style, including a wrought-iron fireplace screen, grand bookcases, Italian antiques, and lush fabrics.

"I wasn't a decorator when I first started consulting on colors for this project with Michael, now with Offenhauser/Mekeel Architects," said Kelly, who formerly focused on art projects. "This wonderful house made a decorator out of me, and launched my design career."

When they began the project, Kelly and Mekeel were faced with flaking orange stucco, a leaking roof, and a poorly detailed kitchen and bathrooms.

"Wright was not around when the house was being completed, and parts of it look like a 'contractor's special' and very banal," Kelly recalled.

"We softened down the colors," said Kelly. "For such an historic house, the furniture and all detailing had to be true and respectful to the architecture. We started from scratch, keeping it very simple."

Kelly ordered Jean-Michel Frank-style sofas, and introduced a pair of Japanese *tansu*, a Japanese embroidery hanging, and sculptural urns with scale and color to stand up to the high ceilings of the living room.

The poured concrete floor, cleaned and sealed, was warmed with Oriental rugs.

A SENSE OF CRAFT
Los Angeles designer
Annie Kelly brought an
arts and crafts feeling to
the bedroom with
vintage textiles, and
lamps and furniture that
were selected to look as
if they had always
belonged with the house.
Plaster walls are by
Christian Granvelle,
a master plasterer.

Kelly engaged decorative artist Christian Granvelle, a master plasterer, to create integral-color plaster finishes on the walls, in tones of umber, rose, and gold.

"The plaster is the color of candlelight," said Annie Kelly, who planned the richly colored walls, waxed and buffed, as a foil for the concrete blocks. The dining room walls were given a tobacco-colored glaze.

"I loved getting to know the house, and having the opportunity to spend hours in Wright's rooms," said Kelly. "To see the way the light moved across the rooms, and seeing Wright's vision, which was so original, was inspiring. Wright was a master of siting."

"NINOTCHKA" WATCHES
Opposite, and left "Grand Comfort" chairs by Le Corbusier, Danish nesting tables, and a glass sculpture from the forties by Kosta are among Patrick Dragonette's favorite pieces in his living room, which adjoins the dining room. A Paul McCobb dining table was made in the sixties for Directional. Honored with silver-leaf frames are two portraits of Greta Garbo by Clarence Sinclair Bull, her favorite portrait photographer. He was head of the MGM stills department for over forty years.

SCREEN GEMS

BENEATH THE ELEGANT EYE OF GRETA GARBO, PATRICK DRAGONETTE DEFINES AN UPDATED ART DECO STYLE

Six years ago, a friend called Patrick Dragonette to tell him that there was a flat to rent in the "Magnificent Moroccans", a legendary group of white stucco duplex apartments with over-the-top "Road to Morocco" architecture, complete with minarets, onion domes, and giant palm trees.

"I had always dreamed of living in one of those buildings, which were built in 1926, the height of Hollywood romantic architecture," said Dragonette, the proprietor of Dragonette, a seven-year-old gallery on La Cienega Boulevard in West Hollywood which showcases mid-century art and furniture.

"The ceilings are coved, and each apartment has colonnades, arches, Moorish-Revival fireplaces, and large terraces," said Dragonette. "They look like a fantasy apartment overlooking the Mediterranean coast in North Africa, or a movie set. I saw apartments like these in matinees when I was growing up, but never

dreamed I might one day inhabit one."

Dragonette drove over to the apartment, fell under the Moroccan spell and rented it on the spot.

"The apartment is right of the border of Los Angeles and West Hollywood, so I sleep in West Hollywood and watch television in Los Angeles," said Dragonette, who shares the apartment with Charles Tucker, who works at the Dragonette gallery.

The apartment is decorated with an elegant collection of mid-century furniture and photography from a variety of sources and countries.

"It's a desire to return to the style of an earlier era, but in a contemporary context," said Dragonette. "Like my clients, I want a bit of Hollywood glamour."

Dragonette is not doctrinaire. He designed a pair of sofas covered in nubby wool/silk fabric from diamond foam and fabric. Beside them are Danish fifties nesting marquetry tables, and vintage "Grand Comfort" chairs

by Le Corbusier.

"We keep the apartment simple, as we share it with two Abyssinian cats, Taylor and Burton," Dragonette said.

In the dining room, a chrome and mahogany sideboard is topped with a Georg Jensen coffee service designed by Johan Rhode, circa 1934.

Above it all hover a pair of thirties portraits of Greta Garbo.

"I fell in love with these portraits," said Dragonette. "They are flawless images of a flawless face. Perfection. Black and white is the ideal medium for such a timeless beauty."

In his gallery, Dragonette sells silver articulated bugs, silver-plated quince branches with crystal flowers, silver-plated magnolia-shaped plates. He also focuses on glamorous, hand-made Art Deco and mid-century furniture and accessories by in-demand designers like Paul Laszlo, Tommi Parzinger, and Billy Haines.

"Billy Haines, of all the fifties and sixties Hollywood interior designers, is my god," said Dragonette, originally from Burton, Ohio. "He created a glamorous décor as well as a wonder-

ful life for his clients. He crafted the finest of the fine interiors and mixed genres and periods with great aplomb. He wasn't trying to do period rooms or pretentious palaces. He had a vocabulary of antiques, but he lightened them up with fine contemporary art, fresh colors, and furniture that was never heavy or over-detailed."

Dragonette, who started his career as a collector, is now in demand for clients who commission interiors for their modernist house in the Hollywood Hills.

"I often start by editing their mid-century collections, and then we move forward creating new décor," he said.

"I like to re-envision decorative vintage furniture and update collections and interiors to make them relevant to today," he said. "I'm not a purist. Designs should be mixed, collections should be the best of the best."

"Hollywood set the standard of glamour in the thirties and forties, and fantastic designs came from this town," said Dragonette. "Money was no object. Beauty, luxury and recollections of time passed were the goal."

DREAMING IN TECHNICOLOR

AT DAWNRIDGE AND HIS OTHER RESIDENCES, TONY DUQUETTE DESIGNED THE ULTIMATE PLEASURE PAVILIONS

Collectors of houses for more than thirty years, Tony and Elizabeth Duquette moved from one romantic caravanserai to a tree house and from a Hollywood dream bungalow to a theatrical studio. At various times, they owned as many as ten houses, including two ranches in Malibu, a studio in West Hollywood, and a Victorian cottage in San Francisco.

Some of their time was spent at their Hollywood Hills house, Dawnridge, where Tony, an acclaimed set designer, interior decorator, and costume designer, and Elizabeth 'Beegle', an artist, attended to the affairs of the Elsie de Wolfe Foundation, entertained a lifetime collection of friends, lectured, designed, and painted. Guests would dine in their exotic Balinese garden, and Tony's dime-store baroque interiors (with enough of the real thing to add verisimilitude) would dazzle even the most jaded art world and design insiders.

In San Francisco, their house on Octavia Street in Cow Hollow was a spangled sanctuary crafted from an 1860 sea captain's house. When Tony was not working on projects for clients like Doris Duke, John and Dodie Rosekrans, designer Adrian, George Cukor, J. Paul Getty, and designing sets and costumes for Broadway musicals or attending an opening at the Louvre, the gregarious couple were sketching, reading or entertaining in their three-story bay-side hideaway.

The San Francisco Victorian, almost completely hidden by a lush Datura tree dripping with fragrant trumpet flowers looked like the romantic Southern town house of a Tennessee Williams heroine. Dawnridge, set in a shady ravine, was like the residence of a London gentleman recently returned from a grand tour of the exotic East with trunks of treasures and dreams of recreating his lost paradise in Belgravia—that is if he was also a close acquaintance of Misia Sert, Elsie de Wolfe, Sharon Stone, Frances Elkins, Syrie Maugham, Ina Claire, and a gaggle of Indian maharajahs.

PAGODAS AND POTTED PLANTS *below and facing page* Tony Duquette conside 18th-century France the apogee of design and civilization, and recreated a Sun K ransom of paintings and festoons for his own pleasure pavilion. Some of the treas from Dawnridge were sold at auction after his death, but even without the gi dolphins, the lacquered secretaires, and soap-stone pagodas shown here, the ro today are still breath-taking, witty, and over-the-

Tony was in San Francisco designing sets and costumes for the opera and ballet when he decided to buy the Victorian house and hire Los Angeles artist Art Fine to paint faux finishes on ceilings, doors, cornices, fireplaces, moldings and windows. The ceilings were traced in elaborate faux marbling with extraordinary detail. A white marble fireplace was painted faux blue marble.

"That was the beginning of my love of *trompe l'oeil*," said Tony, who scorned what he called "the showroom look", the decorating manner that pares decorated rooms down to predictable patterns and obvious design solutions. Duquette loved richness, drama, ornament, individuality and eccentricity.

"I always design my own look. Doing lowest-common-denominator decorating is not my thing," said Duquette, who described himself as designer Elsie de Wolfe's last protegé.

"Art lived in the house for two years. Then we upholstered the walls with antique tapestries and silks. This was the beginning of my quilt syndrome," he noted. Duquette installed mirrors in all rooms to dramatize the space and add a sparkling quality to the walls. Duquette was the master of smoke and mirrors. He even set them in the garden.

"The first time I saw Dawnridge and his Malibu ranch, I was knocked speechless, they were so magical," said Los Angeles photographer Tim Street-Porter, who became a close friend of the Duquettes. "He was an extraordinary individual who reinvented himself every ten years. He decorated rooms, but he was really an artist and set designer. Tony's rooms were sets, very theatrical. He was restless. He couldn't stop. He'd keep adding more, piling on more color, more decoration."

While Fine painted his houses, the multitalented Duquette was away in New York, Paris and, Los Angeles designing costumes and sets for movies (he worked with producer Arthur Freed and director Vincente Minelli), designing gold necklaces (purchased by the Duke of Windsor for his Duchess) and creating elegant interiors for the likes of Norton Simon, J. Paul Getty, and Elizabeth Arden.

"With Art's painting completed, we finally set to work on our houses," Duquette said. His housekeeper would profer Chinese cookies and tea, as the late afternoon shone into the drawing room through Morroccan mirrored jalousies.

"I loved the Victorian style. Then again, I love every style that has richness, texture and history," said Duquette. "I wanted to make my houses look as if the furniture and paintings and our collections had always been here. I didn't want to modernize them at all."

The exterior of Dawnridge, painted pale gray/taupe, never hints of the palatial interiors within.

Past walls layered with paintings and malachite

A TASTE FOR THEATRICALITY
These pages, and following pages
Designer Tony Duquette traveled
extensively in Europe and Asia,
and returned with chests of gilded carvings, jewels, sculptures,
embroideries, furniture, paintings, paper parasols, textiles,
baubles and beads. Bedrooms,
sitting rooms, and an office at
Dawnridge were dressed in
Venetian red silks, Veronese
green velvets, yards of leopard
and ocelot printed carpets, and
exotic bromeliads and orchids.
The sound of windbells in the
garden adds to the Thousand and
One Nights mood. It's entrancing
for some, but minimalists have
been known to tremble and faint,
and dash outside gasping for air.

green alcoves, are a study, luxurious bedrooms, Tibetan tankas, African carvings, silk ikat robes, Chinese lacquered tables, stacks of design books. From this vantage point, Duquette offers a spectacular view over the garden though cascades of hanging plants and orchids.

"Decorating my houses was always a slow process. I kept changing rooms, moving furniture back and forth constantly," said Duquette. "I always decorate as if I were working in the period, rather than merely recreating it. I like to use authentic fabrics and colors, paintings and decorative objects."

Each room is a pastiche of the Duquettes' passions—chinoiserie, gold-leafed trays, Regency mirrors, Louis xv–style chairs, and clusters of pillows made from Balinese fabrics and Japanese brocades. Among the antique Turkish carpets, Chinese screens, Victorian birdcages, rare silk brocades, African carved headrests and Japanese porcelains, New Guinea wood carvings, Duquette offsets his precious collections with theatrical displays of faux coral and fragments of architecture collected on their travels through Asia.

Typical of Duquette's over-the-top style are eighteenth-century Italian-school panoramas, elaborate hand-carved and gilded tabourets with faux ocelot upholstery from Elsie de Wolfe's ballroom at the Villa Trianon in Versailles, Agnes Moorehead's gold-painted tabouret, a baroque-style chest from Frances Elkins.

"Some visitors don't know what to make off all this," said Duquette, who was born in Southern California in 1914 and grew up in Los Angeles and Michigan. "They look around the house and they just don't get it."

Riches for the eye in just the corner of one room might include antique Chinese fabrics, a narwhal tusk, a vitrine of jewelry, painted pagodas from Cost Plus and from China, a Goanese carved stool, Paris green silk cord surrounding an antique English mirror, Japanese lacquer trays, a Portuguese santo, Chinese porcelain bowls, or bright red amaryllis.

"We use all the rooms of our houses," said Duquette. "We have breakfast in our bedroom or in the garden. Lunch is served in the terrace room with sunshine streaming through the window. When it's warm we have afternoon tea among the flowers in the garden. We eat all over the house. We learned that from Elsie de Wolfe, who had trays brought to various rooms of her house in Versailles."

Wherever he was, Tony Duquette and his partner Hutton Wilkinson were at work embellishing, hanging paintings, draping antique embroidered silk, layering shells and faux coral, rearranging tabourets and porcelain, applying faux malachite, and setting up vignettes to a crescendo of clashing colors.

"Arriving at our houses gives us great pleasure," said Tony. "Their feet are firmly on the ground, but they exist to please the eye and embrace all the senses."

A DARING LEAP *This page and facing page* Rudolph Schindler designed his house and studio to accommodate two couples, himself and his wife, Pauline, and his clients, Clyde and Marian Chace. The Chaces were replaced by Richard Neutra and his family in 1925. Walls are tilt-up concrete, hand-formed on site, and spliced with insets of glass for cathedral-like shafts of light. Interiors are Japanese in their horizontal lines and glorification of noble timbers. "The spirit of Schindler warms the works of all of us who were touched by his life," said Frank O. Gehry.

PRAGMATIST AND DREAMER
WITH HIS LANDMARK WEST HOLLYWOOD HOUSE, RUDOLPH SCHINDLER EXPRESSED A DISTINCTLY CALIFORNIA IDEAL

The house sits close to the ground, overlooking an enclosed garden with a lily pond and sheltered terraces. Modest yet visually expressive, Rudolph M. Schindler's studio-residence on Kings Road in West Hollywood is viewed by architectural historians as the first modern house to respond to the unique climate of California, with sliding glass doors offering direct access to out-door terraces and the garden. It eventually afforded a sleeping terrace on the roof, fashionable at the time.

Built on a very limited budget and with great economy of structure, the residence is enriched with a bold handcrafted copper fireplace, waxed concrete floors, and sliding screens that conceal and reveal the beauty of its setting.

From 1922 until Schindler's death in 1953, the building functioned as both Schindler's house and studio. Today it serves as a center for architectural studies and discourse.

Schindler arrived in Los Angeles from his native Vienna, where he had worked with Adolph Loos and Otto Wagner. The architect collaborated with Frank Lloyd Wright on the Hollyhock House, and this Kings Road house was his first independent design in the U.S. With this masterwork, Schindler established himself as a major figure in the history of the modern movement in Southern California.

CHAPTER 2
LA MODERN

IT IS ALMOST EIGHTY YEARS SINCE RICHARD NEUTRA BEGAN
HIS ARCHITECTURAL DIALOGUE WITH THE LOS ANGELES LAND-
SCAPE, AND HIS REVERED WORDS AND BUILT ENVIRONMENTS
INFLUENCE AND INSPIRE A NEW GENERATION OF ARCHITECTS,
ARCHITECTURE JUNKIES AND HOUSE-COLLECTORS.

Fellow emigre architect Rudolph Schindler has also left his soulful
musing on the hearts and minds of Los Angeles architects. A new
generation of cool-seekers like Cameron Silver, is glancing back to
Schindler for ideas on living well and inhabiting the verdant hillsides with fervor and humility.

Modernism is continually evolving, today embracing altruis-
tic residents with a more romantic less rigorous and doctrinaire
edge. Architect Patrick Tighe and his art-loving clients found
inspiration from the iconic Casa Malaparte on the island of Capri
for a painting studio. With brio, architect Mark Rios reinvented an
indifferent box which metamorphosed into a Bel-Air beauty.
The genius of Frank Gehry, now a local hero for his grand, eloquent
titanium-wrapped Walt Disney Concert Hall, like flies like a magical
architecture wizard over Southern California. The experimentation and the lively architectural conversation continue.

THE GENIUS OF SCHINDLER
Opposite, and left
Architect Philip Johnson said that Rudolph Schindler was the most important architect in California of his day and deserved highly the attention given to him by his home-town, Vienna. To his fans in Vienna, can now be added Los Angeles, where vintage afi-cionados Jeffrey Snyder and Cameron Silver have refur-bished a 1930 Schindler house in Los Felix. Beside the open fireplace in the living room is a Schindler reproduction chair. Tall windows pivot open to connect the house to a terrace, to a screen of bam-boo, the hillside, and to the intense Los Angeles light.

SUPER-SCHINDLER

CAMERON SILVER AND JEFF SNYDER RESHAPE A 1930 SCHINDLER CLASSIC INTO A COOL PAD FOR FRIENDS AND DOGS

Vintage fashion guru Cameron Silver was named one of *Time* magazine's "Twenty-five Most Influential Names and Faces in Fashion" in 2002, and things have only escalated from there. Today, his vintage designer label and couture salon, Decades, on Melrose Avenue, is a must-see for fashion-mad red-carpet celebs, style-obsessed vintage junkies, trend-blending fashion stylists, and superstars like Selma Blair, Diana Ross, Nicole Kidman, Renée Zellweger, Cameron Diaz, and Marisa Tomei, along with London heiresses, New York hipsters, and Paris designers.

Just a few miles east of his hot spot, in Los Feliz, is the R. M. Schindler house Cameron and his partner, Jeffrey Snyder, a set designer/actor, acquired in 2001.

"We went looking for a modernist house," said Silver, who grew up in Beverly Hills. "This was the first house we looked at, on the first day of house-hunting. We were lucky to find it, from a small classified ad,

before the MOCA Schindler exhibit created so much frenzy for the architect, and before real-estate prices exploded again."

The house had been built by Schindler in 1930, with rooms added on a lower level in 1939.

"In photos taken in the thirties, the house looks like a spacecraft on the side of a hill, near Griffith Park," noted Silver.

The house is approached from the large steel-reinforced garage (where Silver keeps his 1972 Jensen Interceptor), and entered at mid-level. On the top level is the living/dining room.

Three owners followed the original owner, who was Schindler's insurance agent.

"A kind of prefab modern kitchen and new floors were installed but no one had ruined the essential purity of the house, or Schindler's quirky expression," said Snyder. "He worked from vague sketches, had

eccentric organic concepts that give the rooms a slightly impromptu feeling. We bought it on the spot."

Silver likens his love for the house to his appreciation of vintage couture fashions and their quality, individuality, and timelessness.

"The great thing about vintage fashions is that they're beautifully crafted, never go out of style, and you never get bored with them," said Silver, who, in an earlier life, traveled around North America singing German cabaret, and his favorite, Kurt Weill. "This house is more than seventy years old, yet it feels so right, so fresh, with Schindler still intact."

The complex artistic expression of Schindler, who worked briefly for Frank Lloyd Wright and was a protegé of Adolph Loos, demonstrated his love of fine craftsmanship as well as his use of experimental materials. Schindler's humanistic architecture was a bridge between hard-edged, hard-core International Style Modernism, and warmer and sunnier interiors.

"The concepts of 'comfortable' and 'homey' change their meaning," said Schindler in 1929, of his work. "The comfort of a dwelling lies in its complete control of space, climate, light, and mood, within its confines. The modern dwelling should not freeze temporary whims of owner or designer into permanent tiresome features. It should be a quiet, flexible background for a harmonious life."

Cameron and Snyder agree wholeheartedly with Schindler's manifesto, now some seven decades later.

The partners engaged architects Leo Marmol and Ron Radziner (whose client roster includes Steven Meisel and Tom Ford) to regain the integrity of Schindler's vision, and to focus and refine the renovation.

The architects worked with Schindler's original sketches and from photographs. The kitchen floors were replaced with fir, which Schindler specified. Upgrades, retrofits, and renovation was sensitive, always, to Schindler.

NATURAL SURROUNDINGS
Opposite and right
Architects Leo Marmol and Ron Radziner renovated the former children's bedrooms into an elegant bedroom and study for Silver and Snyder. Photos of the house in 1980 are placed above the built-in bed. Pompeii, a pound Pomeranian, and Hank, a rescued mutt, are a lively part of the family, so furniture in the study, where the dogs hang out, is sturdy and dog-hair colored. The nightstands and headboard in the bedroom are marine-grade plywood, a classic Schindler material.

Snyder designed the rooms with mid-century modern classic furniture that updates each room without overshadowing the architecture. Interior walls were painted a soft white tone, and the exterior, originally ochre, is now a pale sage green.

Silver said that over time they will upgrade and edit furniture and art.

"At the end of the day, the house has to reflect life in the twenty-first century," he said. "We'll take an eclectic approach, so it's going to be Adnet, vintage Hermès objects, Dupré-Lafon furniture, and luxurious French pieces of the thirties and forties that have beautiful handcraftsmanship."

The house project became a collaboration between the partners, the architects, artists, photographers, furniture designers and talented friends.

"We both love this house so much we try to stay home on Sundays and enjoy it," said Silver. "We appreciate the way light falls across rooms, Schindler's idiosyncratic love of imperfection and straight lines."

Silver, a highly respected costume historian and now the darling of the most serious museum curators and vintage collectors, and Snyder, a talented interior designer, travel often, are passionate about their work, and are grateful for the haven their house now affords, along with their commitment to the genius of Schindler.

"There are responsibilities that go along with buying a landmark house," said Snyder. "There's lot of upkeep, and Dave the window washer is a regular visitor. We are constantly editing. We have to honor Schindler, and live up to his expectations. This house is such a cool thing. "

PLEIN-AIR IN BEL-AIR

ARCHITECT/LANDSCAPE ARCHITECT MARK RIOS SETS HIS SIGHTS ON COOL, CLEAN MODERNISM

"I couldn't stand the idea that someone was just going to tear it down," recalled architect Mark Rios of his fifties house, which sits on an acre of canyon land in Bel-Air, with views of the J. Paul Getty Museum and the ocean.

"Here was this nice, clean-lined California modern house, somewhat undistinguished, designed by an unknown architect, just asking to be bulldozed," Rios said. "I knew it was only a Case Study wannabe, but I could see past the peach and turquoise Formica and tattered parquet floors."

Rios loved the site, which has a noble old coral tree with rich red blooms, an evergreen ash, gnarled oaks, walls of bamboo, and blessed privacy with no other residences nearby.

"The house escaped demolition because it had never been renovated or remodeled, and that was exactly what I wanted,"

said Rios. "I didn't want to undo someone else's mistakes, and I planned to keep a sense of its fifties origins."

Rios was mindful of the traditions of modern architecture in Southern California.

"The innovative architecture of Los Angeles in the twentieth century changed people's lives," he said. "Opening a house to the fresh air, steel construction, site-specific architecture, technologically-advanced materials, sustainability, were all ideas that took root here. I wanted to incorporate them into this house, which I was, in effect, recycling."

Rios, a Harvard-trained architect and landscape architect, is a partner in Rios Clementi Hale Studios, a multidisciplinary firm that has designed award-winning residential and commercial buildings, art galleries, children's playgrounds and product, as well as the popular *Terminator 2* theme park ride at Universal Studios, in collaboration with artists including Mary and Bill Buchen, and Allan and Ellen Wexler.

Once escrow closed, Rios tore down walls, opening four bedrooms to create two larger rooms, and improving the floor plan. He took out all windows and installed steel-frame doors and windows on the west-facing view side, and opened up all rooms to the garden. The project took nine months.

"All of the surfaces—walls, ceiling, floors—are continuous from outdoors to indoors," Rios said. A terrazzo floor with speckled pale green, olive green, black and gray tones, runs through the dining room and living room, the entry and kitchen, and out to the loggia,

which has become an outdoor living room.

"Afternoon light on the terrazzo makes the floors alive with light, and it's cool and soft to the feet on a hot day," said Rios.

After returning from Japan, and with the temples of Kyoto dancing in his head, Rio painted the stucco exterior and the tongue-in-groove wall panels pale tones of moss, bamboo, and palest olive green, with a splash of celadon and acid green.

"It was an abstraction of temples I'd seen, which are designed to draw the eye out to the landscape, and which celebrate the connections of buildings and gardens," he said.

The house today is airy and light-hearted, balanced on a raised slab to give it a sense of floating just above the lawn, like a viewing pavilion.

"I've maximized this house, and pushed it to its limit," said the architect. "The interior details are more contemporary and rich, but I've kept the mid-century sensibility."

Like most architects, Rios sees his own house as a design laboratory.

"Now I'm going to paint the interiors a rich chocolate brown and tomato red," he said. "I worked out the colors so that they will be surprisingly peaceful. I will always be taking a new look at the house. I never think of it as being my final word."

LINES LIKE MEDITATION
Facing page, and right
In the Neutra living room, the Egg chair by Arne Jacobsen, 1958, is a curvy contrast to the rigorous, poetic lines of the brick fireplace, and the roof beams. The table is by Isamu Noguchi. The breezeway of the Neutra house, with the elevated garage at left, leads to the bedrooms at right. CJ Bonura and Patricia Moritz planted papyrus in the garden, which they kept austere, as Neutra planned.

FOR THE LOVE OF NEUTRA

WITH DELIBERATION AND RESPECT, AN ARCHITECT SPENDS EIGHT YEARS RESTORING RICHARD NEUTRA'S O'HARA HOUSE

Architect CJ Bonura and his wife, Patricia Moritz, a book designer, did not go looking for a Richard Neutra house. Rather, a Neutra house (aided by an astute real estate broker) found them.

In the mid-nineties, the couple were house-hunting, and the broker tipped them that the iconic O'Hara house would be offered for sale. It was built in 1960 on Neutra Place in Silver Lake, one of nine in the Neutra Colony. It was a three-bedroom house, with a large living room and a deck, nestled into the hillside and sheltered by bamboo. They saw the setting, overlooking the Silver Lake reservoir, and snapped it up before it went on the market. They were only the second owners, after the O'Hara family.

"The house had not been gentrified or modified or changed or modernized in any way," said Bonura, an architect and contractor who specializes in renovating mid-century modern houses in the Los Angeles area. "Nothing had been changed in the house throughout its life. It was designed by Neutra, and closely supervised down to the last perfect detail by his staff. It was polished and then never touched in almost forty years. Even the original carpet and paint were in the house. It was ideal for an architect, just waiting for attention."

Over the years that followed, Bonura and Moritz became experts on the world of Neutra, its materials, its methods, and its timeless beauty.

"I could see that we would be custodians of the house, and at first I was ambiguous about the fact that I would not be creating any new architectural details, additions, or even a new kitchen," said Bonura. "There was a lot of deferred maintenance. All the finishes had to be cleaned and restored. In the end, we touched every surface."

The couple received the original drawings, all blueprints and specs for the house.

"Every one of the Neutra houses has a different flavor and configuration, but each one has the same, consistent Neutra sense and philosophy," said Bonura, founder of Bonura Building. The O'Hara house was the

first Neutra property he acquired and restored.

"Working in the shadow of Neutra has taught me the attention to detail, the discipline, and the fastidiousness required to work on a Neutra design, with total respect for its integrity," said Bonura. "For all their simplicity and lack of pretension, Neutra's houses have everything exposed and it must be perfect. Whenever I had a question, all I had to do was to go back to Neutra's original drawings."

Bonura disassembled, cleaned, restored, and reassembled each piece of the house, working with the same methodical care he takes to restore vintage automobiles.

Neutra Place, where the house is situated, is a mecca for Neutra lovers. The house stands near the Reunion house, the Neutra family house where Neutra's son Dion and his Institute for Survival Through Design are located.

Clarifying and polishing the interior was Bonura and Mortiz's first project.

Bonura made a fortunate find while working on a repair to the roof edge. Neutra's Kaufman house in Palm Springs was under restoration at the same time,

and he was able to acquire a remnant of the corrugated roofing that was custom made for that house.

The interplay of massing and volumes is a source of pleasure for the owners. The genius of Neutra and his staff was to create a harmonious composition of methods and materials. Neutra was the master of simple elegance. He used a single steel column to support the fireplace corner. He emphasized the connection of indoors and outdoors by cantilevering the support beam from the living room out beyond the eave.

By opening each side of the living room to a deck and a terrace, Neutra planned cross-ventilation that draws cool air up from the reservoir and through the house, keeping rooms cool even on hot summer days.

Bonura and Moritz felt a strong bond with Richard Neutra.

"It has been a great experience, living in a masterpiece," said Bonura. "To experience Richard Neutra's great mind at work has been an honor."

ART FOR ART'S SAKE

ARCHITECT PATRICK TIGHE IMAGINES A PRISMATIC ART GALLERY THAT PROVOKES DISCOURSE AND DELIGHT

West Hollywood is known for its dynamic art gallery and design scene.

Along Santa Monica Boulevard, Beverly Boulevard, and the busy streets in between are admired, long-established galleries, and new galleries pumping energy, moving images, ideas, and creativity.

In the leafy streets that circle a quiet enclave just south of Sunset Boulevard, art collector Michael Collins found a mild-mannered 1,400-square-foot bungalow.

Santa Monica architect Patrick Tighe has turned the dilapidated forties house into a sleek new gallery and residence.

"Displaying art was paramount to the program, and all of the interiors were planned with art in mind," said Tighe. "Michael wanted a very monochromatic, pared-down interior that had a somewhat cool commercial feeling, but was very much a home."

Building code restrictions forced the architect to keep most of the footprint within the 4,000-square-foot lot, but he was permitted to tilt the roof planes at an angle to open up skylights into the interior.

Tighe sliced the rectangular building in half on the diagonal. He divided it with a load-bearing diagonal wall across the length of the building, and inserted a wedge-shaped gallery on the east side, and bedrooms, a kitchen, and bathrooms on the west side. The gallery also serves as the living room.

As a gallery/studio, and as a retreat, the building functions with grace and clarity. The art is effectively lit during the day and at night.

"The point was to eliminate windows and maximize the display area," said Tighe. "I've manipulated the space by tipping the roof planes at a sharp angle, which emphasizes the forced perspective of the triangular gallery. "

Steel armatures that cantilever out around the perimeter of the gallery walls provide a framework from

CALM AND COLLECTED
Right Michael Collins
ordered the glass bottles
from a Napa style
mail-order catalog, and
admires their honest sim-
plicity. The wedge-shaped
dining table was designed
by architect Patrick Tighe.
Chairs by Antonio Citterio
for B + B Italia, are covered
in straw-cloth. They're
from Diva on Beverly
Boulevard. The bedroom,
which overlooks the
garden, has a built-in bed
designed by Tighe. The
floor is maple.

which a variety of lighting can be suspended. This system leaves the walls clean and free of distraction. Light in the gallery is also controlled through clerestory lighting, and a large window overlooking the pool and garden.

The only graphic architectural feature in the gallery is a steel-sheathed fireplace and chimney, which supports a mantel/display easel, on which Michael Collins can display a rotation of exhibitions.

"I wanted the focus to be on the art, always, so there are only about a dozen pieces of furniture in the whole house, and they are very minimalist," said Michael Collins. "I want to be captured by the paintings."

A fifteen-foot long tapering steel dining table/desk, designed by Patrick Tighe, stands on a three-legged steel base. It's surrounded by chairs designed by Antonio Citterio for B + B Italia, from Diva.

"The whole space is so austere, and many people ask us how we live here," noted Collins, who shares the place with his partner, Daniel Blanchik, a real estate agent, and their dogs, Olive and Eli. "It's simple and most satisfying. Thanks to Patrick, I feel as if I'm living in a piece of art."

CHAPTER 3
PRIVATE HOLLYWOOD

IT'S AN INDUSTRY TOWN AND EVERY ONE IS DRIVEN TO
SUCCEED BEYOND THEIR WILDEST DREAMS. THOUSANDS OF
SUPER-TALENTED PEOPLE WORK TO CREATE ONE FILM. LIFE
HAS ITS BIG-SCREEN MOMENT AND THEN IT'S TIME TO
RETREAT HOME. HUNDREDS OF INSPIRED MUSICIANS COME
TOGETHER TO MAKE AN ALBUM. AT THE END OF THE DAY,
HIGH-PROFILE TALENT NEEDS PRIVACY. DESIGNERS AND
ARCHITECTS, TOO, CLOSE THEIR DOORS TO SPEND TIME
WITH THEIR BOOKS, THEIR KIDS AND DOGS, THEIR DREAMS.

Antiquaire/designer Rose Tarlow clasps her antique door handle,
locks the door, and shuts out the world. She's free to sketch and
paint in muted interiors of timeless luxury. Interior designer
Suzanne Rheinstein pulls on her chic gardening gloves and stalks
out among her euphorbias and hellbores to get away from it all.
Life is usually dazzling and fabulous in Los Angeles, and sometimes it's necessary to get away from elaboration and intensity.
The surprise is that high-profile people often don't live in houses
that look like glamorous movie sets. They love antiques, charm,
comfort and beauty but they like it real. Sumptuous, yes.
Sybaritic, yes. Family-friendly, absolutely.

TONALITIES AND COMPOSITION
Opposite In her living room, which
has a stone fireplace at each end,
Rose Tarlow has created a superb
tone-on-tone composition with the
balance and composure and timelessness of a painting by Vermeer
or Vuillard. With the simple silhouettes of Knole sofas and club
chairs, she has formed patterns of
light and shade, texture, subtle
color variation, shapes, and
sculpted dark wood. A lifelong
book lover, Tarlow gathers books
on art and philosophy bound in
parchment and leather. Four pairs
of eighteenth-century French oak
doors were incorporated into the
living room design. Tarlow allows
vines to grow into her room, like
delicate green curtains.

THE SOLACE OF BEAUTY

ROSE TARLOW'S BEL-AIR HOUSE HAS BEEN CALLED "THE MOST
BEAUTIFUL HOUSE IN LOS ANGELES."

"My life is a constant search for beauty," said antiquaire
extraordinaire Rose Tarlow, alighting for a brief moment on one
of her gilded "Sir Russell" armchairs in the atelier of the Rose
Tarlow Melrose House in Los Angeles.

"Beauty nourishes me, it fulfills me spiritually. That's why I
design beautiful furniture. It's the reason I am always looking for
objects that move me," said Tarlow.

In the past twenty years, she has turned a successful
antiques company into a multimillion-dollar empire of handcrafted furniture, mirrors, lighting, luxurious leathers, fabrics
for Scalamandré, her own textiles collection, and stenciled wallpapers with the look of faded antique textiles. The Melrose
House furniture and lighting portfolio consists of more than 300
of her designs, and her line is represented in thirteen showrooms

BOOK LOVER Rose Tarlow's living room, which overlooks the garden, is a harmony of natural linens, silk velvets, parchment-covered books, old leather-bound books, Chinese pottery vases, wood carvings, Indian baskets, and wooden floors crafted from old salvaged wood brought over from Europe.

around the country. Tarlow loves to share her knowledge, and currently teaches a master's class in interior design at UCLA.

Rose Tarlow travels to Europe several times a year, always looking for the rare and the *recherché*.

In midwinter, she may be at the historic Kasteel von's-Gravenwezel northeast of Antwerp as a pale ivory sun hovers low in the sky, giving the subdued landscape the look of a faded watercolor. Antiques dealer Axel Vervoordt walks briskly from his study to greet his longtime friend and fellow antiques dealer.

Tarlow has dropped in for lunch at the twelfth-century castle, and to view and admire Vervoordt's art and antiques collection.

"I am a person who loves beautiful things, and I try to be around beautiful objects and exciting art at all times," said Tarlow, glancing at a dramatic Antonio Tapiès painting. She continues on toward a collection of rare Chinese porcelains, smiling, in a reverie.

Tarlow began designing her own collections of furniture thirteen years ago, under the spell of the fine antiques she had acquired and touched and lived with. By constantly rethinking and redesigning antique models, she has attained her singular, polished style.

Tarlow has a particularly fine-tuned sensibility for chairs—the hardest furniture to design—and bestows even a modest dining chair with presence, originality, character, and a distinctive silhouette.

There's the "Puccini" sidechair upholstered in Italian silk, a bestseller. Its carved front legs and boldly arched back give it an air of animation, as if it is about to spring forward. The "Verona" chair, with rich silk velvet upholstery, has gilded legs and arms as finely tapered and turned out as a prima ballerina's.

"My designs tend to be bold," noted Tarlow. "I don't like timid, fussy things."

Rose Tarlow, who was born in Shanghai, has never pigeon-holed herself into one period or style. Her "Étoile" rush-seated sidechair suggests a French provincial inspiration, while the delicate "Cloverleaf" pedestal table, with rich lacquered ebony veneer,

BESIDE THE FIRE *Opposite, and left*
The structure was new, but Rose
Tarlow's art was to use old timbers
and plaster, and to install a handsome old stone floor to give the
kitchen and dining room a sense of
rusticity, age and character. A cosmopolitan and harmonious collection includes Indian baskets,
English and Flemish wooden bowls
and chargers, and an old country
pearwood table. Tarlow has a special affinity with sixteenth and
seventeenth-century country
cabinets, chairs, and tables of
handsome dark woods, which are
polished and cared for to give a
sensuous, heart-warming glow. The
old stone fireplace adds to the
pleasure.

connotes her taste for chinoiserie.

Potential clients are constantly clamoring for her to design their interiors, but she is skittish.

"I think of myself as an antiques dealer," she commented. "I am not really a decorator. I don't really like working with individual clients. I lose control of my creative time."

Tarlow is at her most content when she is searching for and acquiring antiques, or working on her furniture collections—with only her own high standards and acutely sensitive aesthetics to please.

"It's too intense because I take each design decision so personally," she said. "I am a solitary person. I like working alone and making my own design decisions. I have an obsession for buying lovely things, so I occasionally consult on building a collection of antiques and art. I buy and build houses so that I can gather up more antiques."

Tarlow, considered by some a cult figure in the world of design, designed and built her own European-influenced house in Bel-Air.

"I had a vision of this house. I wanted it to seem like centuries-old English or French houses that have not been touched," she said. All of the antique architectural details were found in Europe. She created walls of sanded plaster, installed floors of old wood planks.

Eyes follow Tarlow as she attends an auction, or glides among the burnished rooms of antiques dealer Axel Vervoordt's Antwerp headquarters.

"I know what I like, and my eye goes straight to pieces that are finely crafted, a little eccentric," she said. "Antiques must have quality, whatever their style. Even a collection of old silver or wooden spoons can have superb quality."

Her eye flicks across a Dutch armoire, a Japanese wooden bowl, a stack of old books.

"Everything down to the table linens and soaps in a house must be right. Antiques should have a sensuous quality," she said. "I want to see signs of life and use. If an antique or a stone or shell is provocative, special, I fall in love with it."

When she's not in Paris or New York, Tarlow alights in a grand flat in Belgrave Square, London, and is currently working on her third residence, a village house in Menerbes, Provence.

"I love the village, and my house has a beautiful view," she said. "It's a learning curve. I always love the design process. That's when I'm most alive. Nature is my greatest inspiration. I love trees, anything flourishing and green and beautiful old woods.

I find ideas and inspiration and uplifting things everywhere," said Tarlow.

"Old oil paintings of interiors and watercolors of interiors can be so evocative, and capture a mood and a style wonderfully. Poetry by English romantics like Keats, Shelley, Coleridge and Byron lifts my spirit. Like most designers, I appreciate beautiful, well-proportioned rooms. But some of the most alluring rooms are quiet, contemplative, empty spaces."

A ROOM WITH A VIEW
Opposite, and below Tim Street-Porter and Annie Kelly spend much of the year in their rose-bowered terrace, and with doors and windows flung open to the sun. The chair is French Gothic, and the curtains are silk taffeta. Standard "Iceberg" roses flower on their bedroom balcony from April to November, and honeysuckle scents the air. There's even an outdoor brick fireplace to warm their leafy courtyard.

POSTCARD FROM ITALY

VILLA VALLOMBROSA IS A MINI-PALAZZO WITH A FRAGRANT HISTORY

When photographer Tim Street-Porter and designer Annie Kelly first saw Villa Vallombrosa a decade ago, they knew they wanted to live there.

Hidden in a leafy corner of Whitley Heights, the house was built in 1929 for Eleanor de Witt, an East Coast antiquarian. At first de Witt enjoyed the house as a winter retreat from New York and from 1937 to 1959, she offered it as a romantic rental for film stars, while she lived in a small guesthouse nearby.

"At that time, when Hollywood was in its early stages, you could make a living renting out houses to actors and directors and costume designers who were working on movies in the studios nearby," said Kelly. "This neighborhood has always been inhabited by industry types—screenwriters, producers, artists, and

cinematographers—and most of the houses are in the Mediterranean style."

De Witt commissioned Los Angeles architect Nathan Coleman to design the house, now a designated Los Angeles Historical Cultural Monument.

"The rumor is that Eleanor had done the Grand Tour, and wanted a Tuscan villa, but in its fanciful balconies and tall windows it is more like a Tuscan/Venetian villa," Kelly said. The name, Villa Vallombrosa, was inspired by the sixteenth-century monastery at Vallombrosa, twenty miles outside Florence.

Dame Judith Anderson, Leonard Bernstein, Ben Hecht, photographer Baron Adolf Gayne de Meyer, along with Adrian and his wife, actress Janet Gaynor, were among the fortunate who lived in this timeless

FACE TO FACE WITH HISTORY
Right, top and bottom
Costume designer Adrian
lived at Villa Vallombrosa,
and invited Greta Garbo for
dinner. Eleanor de Witt, right,
built Villa Vallombrosa and in
this thirties photograph,
stands in front of the living
room fireplace, which still
graces the house.

IN THE ITALIAN MANNER *Left*
Kelly and Street-Porter have
decorated the house in the
style of the original Tuscan
palazzo architecture (as seen
through Hollywood eyes). The
chairs are upholstered in vintage Fortuny fabric. The
carved stone mantel is
original to the house.

setting. Greta Garbo was a dinner guest. Omar Kiam, who designed costumes for *Wuthering Heights*, lived there when he worked on the film.

"We were friends with the previous owners, and we used to come to parties in Villa Vallombrosa," recalled Street-Porter. "At one party, we learned that the house was going on the market. We dashed over the next day to inspect it, and even then we knew it was not large enough for us, but we had to have it. In years to come, we would have regretted passing on it."

The exterior of the house, of integral-color hand-troweled concrete, is a trippy Tuscan tour de force. Gothic arched windows, *petite* balconies, and oddly placed windows that appear too small for the rooms within, are circled with steps with overscale balustrades.

"The windows seem tiny from the outside, but the rooms are full of light all day," noted Kelly. The ceilings soar to eighteen feet in some rooms, and at twilight the mood is soft and subtle.

"We dine out on the terrace most of the year," said Street-Porter. The garden is planted with magnolias, Copa de Oro vines, lemon and kumquat trees, and pale pink and white roses, which scent the rooms and seem to cool down the air even on the hottest summer afternoon. On the few rainy days of winter, they

escape to their small sitting room on the *piano nobile*.

"We designed the interiors so that they look as if they've evolved from the twenties," said Kelly. "We have our fantasy of the Mediterranean dream, and so we have our television, fax machines, phones and laptops, and all of today's electronics in miniature form so that they co-exist discreetly with the original historical interiors."

It's a neat balancing act. The couple are devoted to their villa, and are protective of its every rococo curve and sunny corner.

"We've always opened up the house to architecture tours, to cultural groups, and for charity dinners that benefit art museums and cultural institutions," said Street-Porter. "It's important to open the house up to the community, and to let others share our pleasure. It's now almost eighty years old, and it's still enchanting, still magical."

ODE TO FORTUNY Pale taupe Fortuny-inspired wallpaper by Clarence House creates a rhythmic pattern in the bedroom, which has a balcony overlooking the garden and views of the terracotta roofs of Whitley Heights. Garden roses, Mexican paintings found in Oaxaca, a Diréctoire canapé and Fortuny-covered pillows give the room a cosmopolitan air.

INTO THIN AIR *Right, and below* In Los Feliz, Casa Malaparte rises again. Santa Monica architect Patrick Tighe designed a studio structure with a step roof of precast concrete planks which float on a rubberized sloping roof. From the roof deck, both the "Hollywood" sign and the Griffith Observatory are visible. At night, the studio roof is open to the stars and the lights of downtown high-rises.

STAIRWAY TO HEAVEN

ARCHITECT PATRICK TIGHE LIMNS AN ARTFUL STUDIO WITH A
NOD TO THE ENIGMATIC CURZIO MALAPARTE

Only in Hollywood would an architect's client quote esoteric action scenes from a cult movie as inspiration for planned architecture.

The movie in question was *Contempt*, a color-tinted film made in 1964 by Nouvelle Vague director Jean-Luc Godard, starring Brigitte Bardot and Jack Palance.

Bardot burned the screen, but the real star of the film was the Casa Malaparte, the enigmatic cliff-side house/studio built in 1939 on a remote promontory on Capri, by Curzio Malaparte, an artist/writer/political provocateur. The surreal trapezoidal building features a concrete roof staircase that appears to climb into air.

Many architects consider the Casa Malaparte (now a study center) the most beautiful house in the world.

"My client vividly recalled the iconic scenes of Brigitte

ART AND THE MUSE
Opposite, and left For an artist's studio in Los Feliz, architect Patrick Tighe designed a slab-on-grade concrete floor, a 22-foot-tall bookcase, a graphic maple stairway (very Malaparte), and an office/mezzanine. The 20 foot-tall steel-framed door with tongue-in-groove cedar siding opens electronically to provide light and air and inspiration among the palmy Hollywood Hills.

Bardot, blonde hair flying, running down the steps of Casa Malaparte, and said the concept could be a great jumping-off point for his remodel," said Tighe, who was formerly associated with the architectural firms of Morphosis and Frank O. Gehry.

Patrick Tighe's brief was to design a new painting studio, gallery, study/office/loft, and bathroom suite as an addition to a single-story landmark 1947 residence by Wallace Neff in the hills of Los Feliz.

"The existing house is beautiful, very simple, very pure, so I couldn't see violating it with an add-on, in the style of Neff," said Tighe. "I decided on a separate structure connected by a glass gallery, a building with its own integrity, its own ethos. The new studio/loft uses a similar palette of materials and is only partially visible from the front of the house."

For the new construction, Tighe designed a dramatic and complex wedge-shaped building with a precast concrete-staired roof deck and terrace.

"The hillside parcel is wedge-shaped, and the mass-ing of the new building is reflective of the mountainous surroundings, so it's very much at home here," said Tighe. "I've set up a series of framed views as you walk from the glassed-in gallery to the studio and loft, so that the power of the site can be experienced on a journey through the space."

The building, following strict ordinances in this earthquake-prone region, is anchored on nine reinforced concrete caissons which extend thirty to fifty feet into the slope. Thirty-inch grade beams tie the caissons together. The building has a wood frame, with steel components and a gray stucco exterior.

For the double-height studio, direct light filters from the interior stairwell shaft. The second level opens to the roof deck with its grand exterior stair.

The painter can make his way up from the earth to a vast open expanse of roof with sky beyond and a world of possibilities. Curzio would approve.

COLOR HARMONIES
Opposite, and left
Brick steps lead up to the
front entrance of Michael
and Sonya Utterbach's
Hollywood house through
lavender, bougainvillea,
salvia, santolina, roses,
and a Jacaranda tree.
"We selected a subtle
palette of drought-tolerant,
hardy plants that would
do well and have a certain
lushness, even in this desert
climate," said Kate Stamps.
Michael Utterbach found
the eighteenth-century
Portuguese painted tile
wall panel depicting
flowers in a basket in
Puerto Rico. The chairs
and table are Mexican.
The table is draped with
an antique English linen
cloth with inset lace
and embroidery.

BELL' ITALIA

KATE AND ODOM STAMPS PLACE THEIR SUBTLE IMPRINT
UPON A HOUSE NEAR THE HOLLYWOOD BOWL

On a secluded street in the Hollywood Hills, Michael
Utterbach found the perfect house—except that it did
not have quite the gracious proportions he liked. It
would not work for a family, over time.

"It was basically a tiny two-bedroom *casita* with a
kitchen the size of a postage stamp, and a tiny terrace,"
recalled Odom Stamps, an architect and partner with
his wife Kate in Stamps & Stamps, based in South
Pasadena. "It was a rather dark house with low ceilings
and rough plaster walls, typical of houses built around
Los Angeles in the twenties and thirties. It was all
potential."

Working closely with Utterbach on the concept,
Stamps & Stamps created a new entry courtyard,

added a fountain and loggia off the guest bedroom, and
opened up all the rooms. From the outset, they planned
to keep the remodel appropriate to the site, and to its
modest beginnings.

"We always work to make a house as authentic and
natural as possible, not fake, or exploded, or overly styl-
ized," said Odom. "We kept the original architectural
detailing and improved on it, but did not exaggerate it
or make it look grander than it was."

Odom reconfigured the front entrance, raised all
ceilings and covered them, added a new fireplace in the
living room, and gave rooms large new French doors
and windows. Terraces were built around the house,
which backs into the hillside.

A family room was added, and the kitchen was expanded with all new cabinetry that looks like a collection of antique furniture.

"The kitchen was crafted and planned to look as if it had developed over time, rather having the shiny look of a new set piece," said Kate.

Kate, a textile specialist, selected early twentieth-century Scalamandré blue-gray textiles for the living room curtains, and taupe velvet for other windows.

"European houses usually have non-matching curtains, and never look too coordinated," noted the designer. "I used little pattern, and the colors of fabrics are very earthy colors like rust, pewter, olive green, gold, and ocher. Most of the fabrics are vintage, or vintage-looking. It's mellow harmony."

Kate Stamps is adept at rendering fine details to rooms that have a traditional feeling. She also selects the most appropriate

DINING PLEASURE *Below, and left* An eighteenth-century Italian walnut console table stands beneath a mannerist painting of Andromeda chained to the rocks, which Michael Utterbach found in Italy. The eighteenth-century Italian walnut dining chairs surround a seventeenth-century Italian refectory table with later eighteenth-century elements. It was acquired at a Sotheby's auction. The top of the table is a massive slab of walnut.

furnishings, of both grand and humbler provenance.

Velvet curtains from Pottery Barn, which shade the windows in the master bedroom, contrast with an Italian bedcover in silk and linen with elaborate (and rare) soutache embroidery.

The floor in the living room is cherry, newly laid and distressed and swept with sand to look old and original to the house.

The rough textures of the new floor, which was stained a paled-down gray, gave the rooms a more relaxed, less period feeling and kept the house from looking too formal or theatrical.

"In Los Angeles, Spanish Colonial houses traditionally had dark floors, but in Italy and Spain there's less heaviness," noted Odom. "We wanted this house to look more New World than Old World, and less expected than the obvious, over polished, traditional approach."

MEDITERRANEAN MOOD
Opposite, and left A painting of archangel Michael casting out the devil hovers above the nineteenth-century English iron bed and a French burled wood nightstand. A Turkish marble washbasin stands on a custom-made iron stand in the powder room.

Authentic-looking rooms take a lot more consideration and care, said Odom.

"The antiques, paintings and textiles should all be in balance, and rather understated," he said. "No one element should dominate or seem imposed. Michael Utterbach was a great inspiration. He collects antiques and he looked to us to make the rooms in which he would show his trophies coherent, and to live in his dream, but to make it work in real life."

Utterbach collects nineteenth-century books on Italian and Spanish architecture from the fourteenth to the eighteenth centuries, and volumes from the Renaissance to the present.

The walls of the house are smooth white plaster, unpainted.

"It's less decorator-y to leave the walls pristine," said Kate. "A Tuscan or Spanish house would have had simple wall treatments, consistently plain throughout the house, very functional and elegant. They would not have been too thought-out or designed. A house like this should not be too grand or contrived."

Michael Utterbach owns fine tapestries, antique suits of armor, and extraordinary paintings.

"We created the frame for his fine collections," said Kate. "My favorite houses feel as if they have been lived in, beautifully. This house has a presence. It enhances your life."

SCENE STEALER
Right, and opposite
Jennifer Nicholson treasures her dramatic Italian silver-leafed and mirrored table, circa 1850, with its lavish *découpage* images of shells and coral. An English antique cut crystal punch bowl filled with shells, a nineteenth-century French cut crystal bowl, and a pair of twenties glass candelabra add firepower to the glittering tableau. The crystal birdcage chandelier is French. The poodle painting, 1968, by Fernando Botero, was a gift from her father, Jack Nicholson.

A WOMAN OF STYLE
JENNIFER NICHOLSON HAS AN EYE FOR ELEGANT
ANTIQUES OF ENDURING BEAUTY

Afternoon sunshine dances on the gilded arms of a pair of sinuous thirties chairs by Jacques-Émile Ruhlmann and glances across an antique mirrored table, in Jennifer Nicholson's living room.

Cut crystal punch bowls filled with sun-bleached shells and coral branches, flickering crystal wall sconces, and a dramatic mirrored cabinet enhance the sparkling, glamorous effect. But there's a wink-wink quality to this polished scene, and the elegance is cleverly undercut by a painting of a plump white poodle with a pink bow by Fernando Botero, and a series of paintings by Donald Roller Wilson of grinning monkeys in pink tulle skirts.

"I love fine detail and great craftsmanship in furniture—and wit in art," said Nicholson, a fashion designer who founded her own fashion company, Jennifer Nicholson, two years ago. Her designs are sold at Nordstrom stores and at boutiques in Tokyo and Paris. Jennifer, who has been collecting vintage fashions by designers like Emilio Pucci for two decades, is also the founder and owner of Mademoiselle Pearl, a boutique in Santa Monica that sells chic ready-to-wear and vintage fashions.

"In fashion and in furniture and décor, I am always looking for unusual pieces that stand out, and that have stood the test of time," said Jennifer, who is the daughter of Jack Nicholson. Her actor dad gave his daughter the Botero painting.

"A copy, or a 'sort-of', is not going to cut it," Jennifer said. "Good design underpinned with skilled workmanship is essential."

Jennifer has collaborated closely with interior designer (and former antiquaire) Melissa Z. Wallace on her last three houses.

"Jennifer is a fabulous client, and she's very inspiring," said Wallace, whose design firm, Melissa Z. Wallace is based in Los Angeles. "Jennifer studies and collects design books and travels a lot. She's exposed to the best design and the most creative fashion."

Nicholson's Spanish Colonial-style house was built in the fifties. The double-height living room with French doors leading to the garden and a swimming pool was a main attraction.

"Her taste is very eclectic, but we focused on French and Italian antiques and contemporary art," said Melissa. "We had the walls painted a pale creamy

FRENCH EASE *Left* A pair of
moustache-back French
leather chairs, c. 1935, make
an architectural statement in
the bar. Jennifer Nicholson is
a longtime fan of chinoiserie,
and she selected the red
lacquer screen for its subtle
colors and its graphic counterpoint to the curvy chairs.

color, and selected only stellar pieces. There are so many style
possibilities in Los Angeles. Between the design showrooms, the
antiques shops, the crafts workshops in downtown Los Angeles,
the flea markets, auctions, estate sales, and design shops on
every corner, it's essential to be disciplined. It's so easy to be
seduced by something wonderful at the antique galleries along
La Cienega Boulevard or on Melrose Place."

Standouts among Jennifer Nicholson's collection include a
pair of chairs by Jacques-Émile Leleu, from the thirties, with
gilded arms and cream wool damask upholstery. A silver-leafed
tassel table with a smoked glass top complements a thirties secretaire with mirrored panels reverse-etched with images of court
ladies and gentlemen.

"Jennifer is a true collector, and she keeps only the best
examples," noted Melissa Wallace. "Each piece means a lot to her,
and her art and antiques offer a romantic counterpoint to her
busy life."

Melissa is now working on a a chinoiserie office/library for
Jennifer, in *tête de nègre* crackled lacquer with gold-leaf finishes.

"We're making it look like an eighteenth-century study,
beautifully crafted, a little eccentric," noted Melissa. "It will be a
jewel-box, a great place for Jennifer to keep all her design and
fashion books, and her great collections."

FREE AS THE BREEZE
Opposite, and left In Tim Clarke and Art Luna's living room, doors open to the columned balcony and to the garden, flickering with palm trees. A pair of vintage club chairs covered in pale blue linen by Rogers & Goffigon contrasts with a zebra-patterned ottoman, a Brancusi-esque table, a pair of Paris thirties-style chairs, and a stone mantel carved in Mexico. A pair of blue Murano glass lamps are from Modern One. The French chinoiserie fabrics on the pillows are from Brenda Antin. Hurricane lanterns rest beside the 1881 French giltwood mirror.

PURSUIT OF HAPPINESS

TIM CLARKE AND ART LUNA FILL THEIR HOLLYWOOD HILLS HOUSE WITH LUSCIOUS DÉCOR AND FABULOUS FRIENDS

A light-filled Spanish Colonial-style house built in 1936 seems to be the perfect house for interior designer Tim Clarke and hair stylist/garden designer Art Luna. Stone-columned balconies extend along the front of the house, which overlooks a garden with a pool and a putting green. Shady verandahs and terraces connect to the garden and pool and turn the back of the house into an extension of the living rooms and bedrooms.

There's an escapist air to the bougainvillea-twined rooms. Blue-tiled fountains, ficus trees in grand terra cotta pots, orchids, and jasmine turn each room into a conservatory. Only the hum of Sunset Boulevard far

below suggests that this is not Montecito or Morocco.

"When we bought the house, we loved it and thought it needed very little restoration," recalled Clarke, originally from a small town in the middle of Kansas. "It seemed to be in perfect condition, except for the eighties-style peach stucco exterior, but in the end we've improved and touched every surface, and cosmetically enhanced everything."

Art Luna, who tends celebrity hair (Portia de Rossi, Stockard Channing) on Tuesdays, Wednesdays, and Fridays, and gardens every other day of the week, spent months redesigning the one-acre garden, filling it with

A STUDY IN THE HOLLYWOOD
HILLS *Right* Tim Clarke calls his
book-lined room a study, but more
often it's used as a knee-to-knee
dining room. Weekends, Clarke and
his partner, hairdresser-to-the-stars
(and landscape designer) Art Luna
phone their friends then fire up the
lobster club sandwiches and slices
of creamy chocolate cake. They
check the starting time for the
Lakers game, and round up all their
leather chairs around this black
Portuguese table from Brenda
Antin's antique shop. It's an ideal
arrangement for dinner when a
gentle mist hovers over the garden,
or for a summer lunch when the
beamed library is a cool respite
from the sunny terrace just outside.
And if they need one more chair,
Clarke has only to dash down the
hill to West Hollywood to his
design shop, Tim Clarke.

box topiaries, fragrant brugmansias, roses and lavender, and California poppies. The partners jaunt off to England in the summer to tour famous gardens and study borders and clipped hedges, and return to channel their favorite English garden designers, Gertrude Jekyll and Capability Brown.

Clarke and Luna reworked the upstairs library/dining room, which Clarke said is the best-located room in the house. Rich red leather barrel-back chairs from the Tim Clarke Collection surround a black Portuguese claw-foot table from Brenda Antin. Chocolate-brown shelves house design and gardening books.

"The all-purpose study has the best light and the best views, so we spend a lot of time there," said the designer, founder of Tim Clarke Inc., a design shop in a Schindler-designed building near Book Soup in West Hollywood.

GREEN PARADISE *Below, and right* Art Luna has a green thumb—or two. That much is evident from his verdant hillside garden, with its velvety putting green, lavish palm trees, and spills of trumpet vine and jasmine. The columned villa, which appears to command a vast estate, is set on a sheltered hillside moments from Sunset Boulevard.

"We have dinner parties there, and we're knee-to-knee, and it's very cozy for twelve guests, just the way we like it," said Luna.

An English Edwardian faux bamboo dresser, with the original marble top, has been brought into service as a bar, permanently stocked and welcoming. The talented duo entertain often.

"The bar is the first thing that greets friends when they arrive," said Luna. "You mix a cold drink and proceed to the living room, then to the study for dinner, or out to the terrace for a lunch of lobster club sandwiches."

Anyone for lavender lemonade?

GOLDEN AFTERNOONS
Below, and right In the living
room, a Gerhard Richter
painting hangs above a Giallo
Verona marble fireplace
designed by Beeton Associates,
and crafted in Italy. The rosewood bookcase with silver-gilt
trim and the silk velvet-covered
sofa were designed by Thomas
M. Beeton Associates. The pair
of etched bronze tables, c. 1960,
are by New York artists Philip
and Kelvin LaVerne.

SUPERBLY SCRIPTED

DESIGNER THOMAS BEETON AND ARCHITECT RICK ROBERSTON
RESHAPE A THIRTIES MINI-CHATEAU IN HOLMBY HILLS INTO A
GLAMOROUS FAMILY RESIDENCE

"Location is everything in Los Angeles," said designer Thomas
Beeton, who recently completed the renovation of a young fam-
ily's Norman-style house and park-like garden with architect
Richardson Robertson III.

"It was a beautiful location in a two-acre garden, with a rose
arbor, specimen trees, a secluded swimming pool, but it was on
the market for an unusually long time because the interiors were
rather dark," said Beeton. "What my clients acquired, in effect, was
a movie set."

The house was insubstantial, said Beeton, and a series of
vintage rooms had been strung together by previous owners.
There were great bits and pieces, he said, but no coherent architecture holding them together.

Architect Robertson corrected the architecture, enlarged
the house with great sensitivity to the original proportions, and
brought the house up-to-date.

PALE AND PRIVATE *Right, and below* For the guest suite, Beeton selected pale pinks and mauve tones. The eighteenth-century Swedish bed is from Belvedere Antiques, and the nineteenth-century Louis XVI-style marquise is from Evans & Gerst, Los Angeles. In the powder room, Dana Westring painted the Oliver Messel-style murals in a *grisaille* effect. The rope chair is Florentine.

"Our concept was to take the house back to the original bone structure and give it a more consistent French Norman feeling," said Richardson. The owners are Francophiles.

"We had to lighten the interiors and give them a youthful, contemporary feeling," Beeton said. "We all agreed this was not going to be a period French house. My client will wear a couture jacket with a Gap or Marni top. The couple collects the *crème de la crème* of contemporary paintings. I created a certain formality in the structure, a stage, so that Giacometti, Swedish antiques, Picasso and Adnet and Richter and Billy Haines pieces could live together with ease."

Beeton and his clients shopped in Paris for French thirties furniture, the early period for the house. He put together a "look book" with clippings of architectural details, colors, sofa styles, ways of creating atmosphere, curtain designs.

They found Billy Haines chairs, an eighteenth-century giltwood fauteuil from Gore Dean Antiques, a Giacometti cocktail table and thirties Italian modernist chairs. Striped curtains in the living room are luxurious Christopher Hyland Thai silk.

"In the end, with every room redesigned and refreshed the house was given its moment of glamour," said Beeton.

The original conservatory was enhanced with a new lime-

INSIDE OUT *Opposite and below*
Thomas Beeton decorated the
glittering chandeliered conservatory and the outdoor dining
room with as much glamour and
ease as indoor living rooms. Here
the family can enjoy breakfast,
gather friends for cocktails, or
relax after a Sunday swim or late
dinner. The outdoor furniture
was designed by Thomas M.
Beeton Associates and crafted by
Leslie Curtis, Los Angeles.

HOME ALONE *Following pages*
The swimming pool, which was
updated and redesigned, is in a
quiet glade a short walk from the
house and is completely private,
quiet and peaceful. A fountain
splashes, birds chirp, children
play. The cares of the world
are far away.

stone floor and skylit roof. It's graced with an American chinoiserie table found in Boston.

At night, with candles lit, friends gather for drinks overlooking the lush landscape. They can relax for a moment on a
rattan chair or a chair from Brenda Antin or wander into the
moonlit garden.

"The new dining terrace was designed for entertaining, both
day and evening," said Beeton. There's a table that can seat ten,
a wicker sofa and chairs made by Leslie Curtis surrounding
a fireplace.

"The greatest pleasure is to see how the owners have brought
the house to full bloom by living in it," said Beeton. "The family
are in the hotel business and they entertain often and it seems
rather effortless."

Beeton and Robertson have succeeded in their mission.

"We didn't try to erase the past, but rather highlighted it,"
said Beeton. "This house was designed to be enjoyed for a
long time."

CHAPTER 4
HOLLYWOOD DESIGNED

IT'S A CLASSIC HOLLYWOOD STORYLINE. EVERY HOUSE, EVERY COTTAGE, EVERY PEDIGREED PROPERTY COMES WITH ITS OWN BIOGRAPHY, ITS OWN STAR CREDITS, ITS ANECDOTES, GOSSIP, AND LEGENDARY DESIGNERS.

"Norma Talmadge lived here", "Charlie Chaplin slept here", "Judy Garland entertained guests beside this tree", "Cedric Gibbons designed the staircase" and even "Charlie's Angels" was filmed here". Golden-age stars, directors, set decorators, and even costume-designers hover like friendly ghosts over some of the best houses from Whitley Heights and Bel-Air to Santa Monica and Pacific Palissades. New generations of stars and designers are now bestowing magic and style on interiors and giving them fresh cachet, new light. Leading designer Michael Smith works with A-list stars, financiers, and directors to create elegant, polished and personal decor with a refined sense of Hollywood design history. Tim Clarke, with his blond-surfer good looks, roves through Los Angeles design decades with ease, forgoing movieland illusions for real comfort, practical ease. Design ingenuity brings new life to houses basking in the Hollywood sun, and the script is constantly being rewritten.

GRACIOUS WELCOME
Below, and right An English Regency neoclassical sofa graces the living room, which has a Georgian pine mantel. Suzanne Rheinstein creates gentle harmony with a Victorian sofa upholstered in smooth wool fabric, and a pair of French chairs upholstered in silk velvet. The curtains, in silk/linen, have an elegant air but are not overly formal. Above the fireplace is a late seventeenth century English oil painting. The living room and the dining room are on the front of the house.

POLISHED TO PERFECTION

DESIGNER SUZANNE RHEINSTEIN COLLECTS THE RARE AND THE BEAUTIFUL IN HER FAMILY'S HANDSOME WINDSOR SQUARE RESIDENCE

"The best thing my husband ever did was bring me to Los Angeles," said designer Suzanne Rheinstein. "That and deciding with me to acquire our house in Windsor Square, which I love more each year."

Fred and Suzanne Rheinstein's superbly symmetrical brick house stands on a street lined with palm trees, and to the north the "Hollywood" sign is visible as Suzanne heads in the morning to her trend-setting West Hollywood design and antiques gallery, Hollyhock.

Suzanne founded her skylit shop (formerly the studio of Tony Duquette) fourteen years ago. It has become a magnet for designers in the know, clients from around the world, an impressive group of lecturing authors and art historians, New York jewelry designer Mish Tworkowski and his latest creations,

BIRDS IN PARADISE *Below, and left* Suzanne and Fred are interested in lively, creative, inspired people, so they're natural and warm entertainers. In their dining room, with gold-framed watercolors of birds and pale golden silk curtains, they'll arrange tables that shimmer with William Yeoward's handcrafted crystal and English bone china.

accomplished artists, and collectors of rare design books and vintage fashion illustration.

"I adore design history, and I've enjoyed creating a dialogue between interiors designers and design authorities around the world," said Rheinstein.

At home, too, Suzanne, a generous supporter of the Garden Conservancy and many arts and museum groups in Los Angeles, gathers a lively colloquium of talented and attractive people to dine, to stroll in the garden, and to enjoy the remarkably comfortable and elegant atmosphere she has arranged. It's a superb setting for large musicales, and for a small *tête-à-tête* on a summer afternoon to plan an upcoming benefit.

The house, which they acquired in 1980, was built in 1914 by the Milwaukee Building Co., which later became Meyer and Holler, the great classical revival architects of Hollywood.

"The house was built in a bean field for families moving west from downtown Los Angeles," noted Suzanne. It was one of the first in the area, on streets that are now full of attractive family houses, built on a human scale. They are large and gracious, but not overbuilt.

The Rheinsteins' house is in the Colonial Revival style, in

red brick with white trim and Charleston green shutters. Red oaks, liquidambar, and rosa banksiae surround the property.

A large foyer, a sunny living room, a library, a dining room, a kitchen/butler's pantry/service porch, all on the ground floor, make it comfortable for quiet family evenings at home, and versatile for chattering groups of arts philanthropists.

"The house had not had many owners, and one family had lived here for fifty years, so it was in wonderful shape," said Suzanne, who was originally from New Orleans.

The living room is an elegant ensemble of an English Regency sofa, French chairs, and family heirlooms. A large contemporary collage by Charles Garabedian hangs near the windows.

"Contemporary art works well here, and I like the contrast with the Chinese painted wallpaper panels, and our portraits of doges," said Rheinstein. She has a special fondness for furniture and art from the first quarter of the nineteenth century, for its fresh and graceful style.

"The craftsmanship in the early 1800s was marvelous and often quirky," said Rheinstein. Her English table carved with dolphins with baroque curving tails enliven a series of *verre eglomisé* portraits and *coquillage* designs crafted by English and French women in the eighteenth century.

"I'd rather have fewer things and better things," said Suzanne. "And I like everything to be beautifully maintained. It matters to me that the floors glow softly, that the silver gleams, and that the linens are neatly pressed."

In the summer, hardwood floors are hand-waxed and buffed, and left bare for coolness and simplicity. In winter, out come the Oriental rugs.

The Rheinsteins are also avid gardeners. Behind the house is a pool house and swimming pool. A Chinese weeping elm and the creamy, scented flowers of brugmansia add character and delight.

Behind a pleached fence of five quince trees, four kinds of figs, and a row of potted citrus, including kumquats and satsumas, are pastel clouds of Abraham Darby, Cherokee, and Rêve d'Or roses.

"I grow the roses for their fragrance, and also for cutting for the house," said Suzanne. "The garden, designed by Judy Horton, gives me enormous pleasure. It's all completely organic, with very good, healthy soil."

During the summer, the Rheinsteins entertain often.

For a dinner or a cocktail, they'll have a pianist playing bouncy show tunes, and guests gather round the piano singing along. No one wants to leave.

"We'll be in this house forever," Suzanne said. "It's the way I like to live. The scale is perfect. We use every room. Fred and I will take dinner trays into the study, or set ourselves up in the dining room on a Saturday evening. I thank my husband every day that we live in Los Angeles."

CARVED IN STONE *Below*
The front entrance of the
Talmadge villa has a carved
sandstone entry and
twenties lanterns from
Montecito installed by
Balbes. The Italian stained-
glass window, depicting
cherubs holding a crown,
was repaired and restored to
its original glory.

WATER OF LIFE *Opposite*
The swimming pool at the
back of the house faces the
hills of Los Feliz. Swimmers
and sunbathers enjoy
views of Hollywood and
downtown Los Angeles, the
San Fernando Valley, and
Pasadena and the San
Gabriel Mountains.

HOLLYWOOD GLORY DAYS

A GILDED TWENTIES MANSION WITH THE GHOSTS OF NORMA
TALMADGE AND JIMI HENDRIX REGAINS ITS ALLURE

High in the hills of Los Feliz, with a view of the snow-capped San
Gabriel Mountains and the sunlit towers of downtown Los
Angeles, stands a 1926 replica of a seventeenth-century Italian
villa. After gathering dust for the last forty years, the villa
has recently been restored and revived by Xorin Balbes, a Los
Angeles designer/real-estate developer who specializes in
restoring architecturally significant properties.

His Norma Talmadge estate, also known as The Cedars, had
been developed in 1926 by Madge and Ralph Bellamy, silent
screen actors, on fifteen acres. They not only used plans inspired
by Florentine palazzi, they also brought Italian craftsmen to
make stained glass windows, carve stone, stencil the vaulted and
beamed ceilings, create the *bas* relief plasterwork (including 120
lions), and paint convoluted fantasy ceilings in the bedrooms and

GAME OF CONTRASTS
Previous pages Just as modern Italians who live in Milan or Florence love to spark their historic interiors of a sixteenth-century palazzo with edgy contemporary furniture, Balbes juxtaposed a pair of grand-scale raspberry suede Doma sofas and custom-crafted brushed stainless-steel cubes against walls washed in an ocher tint, and gilded columns. Two-tiered forged iron light fixtures, hand-crafted in Los Angeles, hover above the newly installed ballroom floor. The gilded wood Venetian fire-screen was acquired in San Francisco. The Baccarat chandelier in the solarium is original to the house. It even survived Jimi Hendrix.

DETAILS, DETAILS *Opposite, and left* Xorin Balbes pays fanatical attention to detail, and has a team of craftspeople who are experts in fine gilding, plastering, carving, faux painted finishes, and historic restoration. The plaster lion above the tiled and plastered fireplace, the vaulted ceiling, as well as gilded finials, carved ceilings and ironwork, all received lavish, historically correct attention. The fireplace in the study is original to the house.

bathrooms. Each room is like a stage set, waiting for Greta Garbo or Norma Talmadge (or the silent stars, Madge and Ralph) to make a walk-on appearance.

In the thirties, screen legends like Valentino and Norma Talmadge stayed at the 10,800-square-foot house. In the sixties, Jimi Hendrix and Rod McKuen were said to be residents, presumably not at the same time. In the mid-sixties, the villa had been acquired by a university professor, a rare book collector who used it as his book repository.

"I saw a newspaper advertisement and noted that the house had not been on the market since the sixties," said Balbes. "I rushed over. The house was filled, crammed and jammed with books. I couldn't walk down the hall to view the dining room. The professor and his wife had bought the house in 1965 for $130,000, and had never lived in it. He'd come and sit and read and study, and go home."

Balbes convinced the professor of his passion for significant houses, and his bona fides. The designer had just spent two years restoring the 1926 Sowden house by Lloyd Wright, Frank Lloyd Wright's son.

"The house is fabulous but I had to repair the roof, restore the garden and pools, replace the plumbing, and correct the disastrous decrepitude," said Balbes, who brought in a fine-tuned team of sixty craftsmen, who worked on the house for a year.

"All the ceilings were cleaned and walls were plastered, and floors were replaced," said Balbes. "It's a glamorous house but before I rescued it, the glamour was gone. In its place was pseudo-glamour, brassy and glitzed-up"

"The gilded columns and the ceiling and decoration in the ballroom and the solarium were bright 24-karat gold, screaming bright," said Balbes. "I had to restore a sense of elegant age to the house. I toned the gilding down and cleaned it, and then antiqued it to feel its age, not glitzed up. The villa had been built for entertaining, for balls and masquerades, so I restored the fantasy."

Balbes, originally from Michigan, came to Los Angeles to work on AIDS-related fund-raising. He now supports a nonprofit group that works on peace projects.

Next on his design and restoration project list is a fifties post-and-beam house (Case Study house in style), a historic Hollywood apartment building, and a 1927 Art Deco former bank building.

"I'm addicted to holding on to the architectural history of Hollywood," said Balbes. "We must keep these buildings and protect all the strands of our culture."

MALIBU LUAU

ON THE PACIFIC COAST, INTERIOR DESIGNER KERRY JOYCE GOES HAWAIIAN FOR AN ACTOR AND HER FAMILY.

If you love escaping to the beach and can take the roller coaster of hard-core curves along Sunset Boulevard at rush hour (or are blessed with a car and driver) Malibu is the place for you. First there's that feeling of endless summer, and the sea air, the vibrant light reflecting off the Pacific Ocean, and the allure of living in beach clothes every day of the year. Not too bad.

All that was part of the attraction of a shingled beach cottage for a noted actress, her husband, and their three young sons. The location was right, the orientation was perfect, but there were problems with the existing house.

"The original house had been built in the sixties, and it was just awful," said Los Angeles interior designer Kerry Joyce, whose forte is creating atmospheric houses that feel as if they've always stood in just that place. "I wanted it to look like a classic

MAUI MOWEE *Opposite, and left* In a sunny guest room, Kerry Joyce designed a printed hemp fabric for the palm-y headboard. Vintage pillows, lanterns and posters were scooped up in Honolulu. Joyce's mantra: keep the backgrounds and the linens white, then punch in the accent color. Rainbow-colored cocktail lanterns, souvenirs of weekend parties, are attached to the ceiling in the guest cottage dressing room.

beach house, like the ones you see in Nantucket, the kinds of places you only visit in summer."

First he had to banish the brown, orange and "very un-beachy" shack that stood on the perfect site in the ideal Malibu location. He tore it down to the studs.

"Initially, I was thinking Nantucket for the shingled exterior, and then for the interiors my clients and I were inspired by Hawaii and I went color mad," the designer said. "We mixed it up and found some great vintage posters and fabrics at flea markets. I ordered very good upholstered pieces in the designer showrooms of the Pacific Design Center."

The result is eccentric, relaxed, and a great deal of fun.

"The key to designing a beach house or a country house is to keep the spirit simple and pure and playful," said Joyce, who collected furniture and accessories in

Hawaii for bedrooms and bathrooms. "It's too easy to fall into seaside clichés. There should be some formality to the structure, but you have to design rooms so the owners don't worry about every little inch of fabric or carpet."

Joyce thought through the daily life of the house, encouraging an improvisational air. He has now designed three houses for these clients, and they love to bounce ideas around, challenge, and surprise each other.

"A beach house in Malibu should not be too pretentious," Joyce said. "Furniture and slipcovers must be appropriate for hot weather, as well as for cool evenings. If you want to relax in a bathing suit or shorts, or eat Chinese takeout in front of the television, then the sofas and tables and chairs must be perfect for all of that. Kids may want to run through the house with their surfboards. And you should be able to use all of the rooms, at any time.

SHELL GAME *Left* Interior designer Kerry Joyce was once a set designer and an antiques dealer. He edged into decorating, encouraged by his clients. How he has a thriving design business and an elegant furniture collection available at national showrooms through the prestigious design firm, Dessin Fournir. For a family house on the coast in Malibu, Joyce let his design become a dash more playful. Working with scallop shells by the bushel, he ornamented a cabinet, doors, ceilings and beams worthy of a villa on Capri. Here guests are taken back to carefree days beside the sea. And if it's raining (only in winter) the shell-adorned cabinet opens to reveal video games, a television, and all the electronics any child could want.

Here, you just sweep up the sand. No problem."

Floors are painted white, with sea-grass matting rugs.

The house on the water has been a roaring success. Guest rooms have views of the sea, the boys have their own bathroom with space for surfboard storage, and the parents have enjoyed Joyce's careful planning, balanced with wit and whimsy.

"I've splashed the color around, but only in accents and dashes," he said. "The white background is soothing, and you've got the endless ocean out the window. Vivid color should not compete with this spectacular view."

DAILY RHYTHM
Right, and below "I gave the living room double-hung windows and opened it to the views and the garden," said Kerry Joyce, who arranged Jami Gertz's collection of California pottery along the mantel. A wool sisal rug and miniature chairs are intentionally child-friendly. A gold-framed mirror strikes a dramatic pose beside a Biedermeier-style chair. The windows were left bare, screened by stands of oaks and oleanders which are green year-round in Southern California's eternal spring.

THE WHITE HOUSE

FOR ACTOR JAMI GERTZ AND HER FAMILY, KERRY JOYCE LIMNS A HOUSE WITH FRESH, WHITE ROOMS THAT OPEN TO AN OAK-SHADED CANYON

Interior designer Kerry Joyce is a purist and a perfectionist. That's clearly demonstrated in the clean lines of the refined and rather self-effacing rooms he plans, which have an almost Shaker-pure elegance. He insists on authentic and intelligent plans, rigorous examination of every aspect of the décor, and appropriate furniture arrangements. And he takes the taste for traditional styles as a given for most of his Los Angeles clients.

"Experimental design is great, but my clients always want a house that works, that is aesthetically pleasing, rather than challenging", said Joyce, a graduate of New York University's theater school who won an Emmy award for set decoration. "People who come to me for interior design and furniture don't ask for hard-edge modern. They want a timeless feeling, a sense that a house is genuine, well thought-out, not faked out."

His first assignment gave him the experience and the con-

fidence to found his own firm, Kerry Joyce Associates, Inc., and to commit himself to a career in design.

"Jami Gertz and her husband Tony Ressler came to me for help in planning and making sense of their new Los Angeles house," Joyce recalled. "This was my first commission where I was responsible for the architecture, the interior and the furniture."

Joyce had previously been the founder of a Los Angeles store, Designer Resource, which sold architectural detail, including antique columns and mantels, plaster moldings, and the kinds of trim, frames and wood moldings that add character and depth to new construction.

Plans had been drawn up for the house, which is set in a leafy canyon near Beverly Hills, and building permits had been obtained. It was up to Joyce to give the new 5,000-square-foot house life, working with the pre-existing footprint.

"This house was in a great location with valley views and giant live oaks, but it felt like a basic tract house," Joyce said. "I reconfigured the completed floor plan and gave some rooms a twelve-foot ceiling. My challenge was to take away the 'brand-new' feeling and to give it an informal but highly detailed look."

In the living room, Joyce played a game of contrasts with a pair of Biedermeier-style fan-back chairs, a French-polish mahogany coffee table with gracefully curved legs, and a gold-rimmed Federal mirror over a simple mantel. Entry to the room is through a beautifully composed doorway framed with simple columns.

The forties-style cotton chintz selected for slipcovers on the living room sofas was used in reverse to fade out the pattern of leaves and ribbons.

"I generally don't use patterned fabrics as they tend to be too assertive and draw your eye away from the overall look of a room," Joyce said. "But if you work with the reverse of a textile, the pattern is still there but it's softer."

Floors throughout are hardwood, and in the entrance he has fashioned a French limestone floor with black inserts.

"I'm a modernist at heart, doing traditional interiors," said the designer. "I simplified the architectural details throughout, without obliterating them. It's pure but with character and refinement."

Joyce likes to make his clients happy.

"I want interiors to feel good, not just look good," he said. "A house can be laid out a thousand different ways, but the architecture must make subliminal sense. Things have to be in the right place. It should feel substantial and real, even when it's empty. The bones, the background must be right."

Joyce composes rooms like completing a painting.

"I work to create the look, to make a room well-balanced," he said. "I exaggerate the height of a ceiling to create drama. I get the box right, and then layer the shapes within it. I select the colors last, and I seldom use pattern other than stripes. Most chintzes make me gag. They're too much. They take away from the architecture and the balanced composition."

Joyce admits to being obsessive.

"I care about everything—proportion, line, the view, traffic patterns, finishes, contrast and variation within a room, comfort, use, appropriateness," he noted. "A good room is successful if after everything is in place, it's at rest, if it's tranquil. Rooms should take you out of the mundane and ordinary. In a perfect room, life is in balance, you're transported."

WELCOME HOME *Left, and opposite* Designer Peter Dunham banished a goofy shingled Swiss chalet exterior and gave it a more stylish, dramatic look with Mediterranean flair. A new arched loggia entrance with stone statuary and sculpture, now leads guests into the house.

ROOM AT THE TOP

DESIGNER PETER DUNHAM RE-IMAGINES A 'RICKETY BOX' INTO A GLAMOROUS HILLSIDE HAVEN, A WINDOW ON THE WORLD

Hollywood Hills houses don't always come neatly packaged or camera-ready. They do have breathtaking views and are blessed with klieg-light illumination in the ultrabright Southern California summer, but often vertiginous sites and low-down developer instincts collide to produce surprisingly ticky-tacky buildings.

Above Sunset Plaza, on a steep site that would have been impossible to build on fifty years ago, Los Angeles designer Peter Dunham discovered a diamond in the rough.

"Developers were climbing further and further up these perpendicular hillside lots, and this odd-looking house, built in 1975, was the result," said Dunham.

"The exterior at street level was some kind of wacky Swiss chalet concept, one of those follies Los Angeles is prone to," said Dunham, who was born and educated in Paris, and has lived in Morocco and London. "Below, the rooms dangled over the hill, totally illogical and uncomfortable."

The designer and his partner, Peter Kopelson, a dermatologist in practice in Beverly Hills, could see past the "Neapolitan shantytown" conglomeration of rooms and makeshift architecture.

"We bought it for the fantastic location, which has views for days over Beverly Hills and West Hollywood to the lights of downtown Los Angeles," Dunham said. "We could see the ocean, and it's a fast drive down to Sunset Boulevard."

The partners intended a quick fix, a cosmetic job, for the house.

"The house had not been repaired since the last major earthquake in the early nineties, and in reality, it needed a lot of work to make it work for us," said Dunham, who had formerly worked in New York for fifteen years. "We discovered space beneath the house, and over months of construction, added guests suites with a private entrance. We reclaimed a former basement space and turned it into a living room with a high ceiling."

Dunham changed the layout so that the living room was downstairs, the bedrooms were upstairs, and rooms had easy transitions. Both the living room and the kitchen now open to a sunny terrace sheltered by palms, mimosas, and citrus trees. Now the rooms and

views feel like Tangier, rather than Swiss Miss.

"We've both traveled, in the Orient and North Africa and Europe, and I wanted to recapture that seductive, happy, crickets-chirping, birds-whistling, palm trees rustling kind of feeling here," said Dunham.

"I grew up in Paris and I had such a fantasy of Los Angeles and Hollywood, and I wanted to create a bit of that dream," said Dunham, who curtained the windows with hand-block printed cotton muslin fabrics of his own design, and brought in vintage movie-theater light-ing, old hand-carved doors and beams, and reclaimed pine floor planks to create the cross-cultural setting of his boyhood imagination.

"In my design, I like to assemble interiors," said the designer. "For myself, not my clients, I like to have things coming and going, and to experiment with dif-ferent arrangements of furniture. I have a vast collec-tion of chairs, tables, paintings, lamps, and rugs, art and objects I've collected over the years all over the world, including Los Angeles flea markets, Moroccan souks, and London antiques dealers."

Dunham is a lifelong, consistent collector.

"We've got hand-me-downs, rare and precious things, and things I've found driving down La Brea Avenue," said Dunham. "In Morocco or India or Europe, I'm always looking for architectural fragments, salvage, doors, or carved mantels that I can incorporate into new architecture. In the master bedroom, I've used a pierced and curved window from Marrakesh on the bal-cony. It added so much character, took away the newness."

The inveterate collector found twenties light fixtures, handcrafted grillwork from demolished Spanish-style houses in Pasadena, and quirky sconces and brackets that would add texture and charm to the house.

HILLSIDE HEAVEN *Right, and below* Peter Dunham shaped an elegant roof terrace that has all the grace and accoutrements of a comfortable living room. The décor vibrates to the designer's favorite Euro-African beat. Vintage Kreiss Collection *chaises-longues,* an Oriental rug, Indian paisley prints, a bar swathed in a vintage *suzani* fabric, and a sheltering trellis wall make this ideal for early evening drinks, Saturday afternoon chats, or quiet time with stacks of books and design magazines. Below a book-filled hall invites lingering.

Dunham also channels his favorite, iconic designers with an apricot velvet Billy Baldwin slipper chair, a fern-patterned fabric by Elsie de Wolfe, armchairs and a faux-leopard rug by Syrie Maugham, and a crimson slipper chair by Valerian Rybar. But he's not a design snob. Downtown Manhattan junk shops, auctions, estate sales, and the San Diego flea market all yield treasures for Dunham, who has a finely tuned eye.

"I'm always open to great, well-designed, and eccentric things, no matter their provenance," the designer said. "All of our furniture and our stuff comes with a great story and has special meaning to us. This house has been a fantastic experiment, and, in the end, a dream project."

VIRTUOSO PERFORMANCE
Opposite, and right It's a tiny
bungalow in West
Hollywood, the former
dressing room of star Norma
Talmadge, but you'd never
know it after design Martyn
Lawrence-Bullard had pulled
out all the stops. A time-
faded Flemish *verdure* tapestry creates a sense of endless
landscape, and a convex
mirror dazzles a guest into
thinking this is a Belgravia
pied-à-terre. Pillows with
bullion fringe, embroidered
silk velvets and tapestries
enrich his *mise-én-scene*." I
travel the world to find rare
textiles and antiques that
have eccentricity and
character,"said Lawrence-
Bullard. "A designer is only as
good as his sources—and his
bravado and daring."

AN ENGLISHMAN IN...LOS ANGELES

A FORMER ACTOR GAINS STAR QUALITY AS A WILDLY POPULAR WILDE-QUOTING INTERIOR DESIGNER

Martyn Lawrence-Bullard is a classic Hollywood success story...in a deliciously twisted way.

"Yes, I'm a true Hollywood story, in reverse," he said. "I came here from London twelve years ago to be an actor, and it didn't work out, and by chance I became a decorator, who then became a television host presenting star's homes and decorating on British television. I've come full circle."

His design career is buzzing. Lawrence-Bullard has his own interior design firm, Martynus-Tripp, with partner Trip Haenisch. He's also starring in his own new reality show about his star clients in Los Angeles for BBC America, and in his few milliseconds of spare time he's designing candles and furniture and more clients are ringing his bell.

"My taste is eclectic, ebullient, varied, and client-specific, and runs from Moorish lanterns, Anglo-Indian antiques, Moroccan and Syrian tables, early nineteenth-century campaign furniture and Indian textiles for myself, to Balinese, Andy Warhol, Tuscan villa, Elsie de Wolfe revival, and total glam for my clients," said the designer, whose own cosmopolitan and high-calorie hous-

es reflect his restless creativity.

In his dining room, Lawrence-Bullard lays out a panoply of favorite English antiques and both shabby and chic treasures from the Marché Paul-Bert at the Clignancourt flea-market in Paris. There are Picasso etchings, Georgian silver, tissue-thin Oriental carpets, glam Venetian gilded frames, and rich and eccentric *objets* covered in ostrich, alligator, zebra skin, and galluchat from various provenances and assorted centuries. The Grand Tour lives on.

"All beautiful things belong to the same era," said Lawrence-Bullard, quoting Oscar Wilde. "I mix precious things like a Grinling Gibbons carved fireplace surround and flea market trophies and a rare Flemish tapestry with things from Crate & Barrel or the Rose Bowl and it all works because they have intrinsic quality and style."

As a stage set for dining, nineteenth-century English and French paisleys are a fine backdrop for Coalport china dinner service depicting Staint George slaying the dragon, a family heirloom.

His antique English dining chairs, covered in vintage

YOU'RE INVITED *Right, and below* The designer is an enthusiastic entertainer who has been known to offer an exploding (almost) chocolate cake for Vidal Sassoon, cocktails for Christina Aguilera, or a glamorous dinner for Patti LaBelle (all clients), and his dining room has been the setting for serious dining (and singing). Lawrence-Bullard has two rules on dining rooms: all lights must be on dimmers, and candlelight should be used every night, to great effect. The silver cornucopias and the walrus-tusk epergne give the table an English air.

Fortuny fabrics, have Lawrence-Bullard's family crest painted on the back.

For the designer, each room is camera ready, with layers of color, antique textiles, collections, paintings, trunks, pillows, and books added for dramatic effect. In the dining room, a French walrus-tusk *vermeil epergne* and a nineteenth-century English cornucopia emblazoned in silver catch the light.

Lawrence-Bullard's house, with its name-dropping history, soaring ceilings and quirky corners, matches his own better-than-real-life story.

The oldest residence in West Hollywood, it was built in 1918 as a star dressing suite for Norma Talmadge by Charlie Chaplin, when the Chaplin studio was nearby.

After the studio closed, the cottage, with its Cape Cod-style shutters, was converted into a residence for Tallulah Bankhead. Judy Garland and Dorothy Parker lived there over the following decades.

"I found the house by a complete fluke, from a chance conversation," said Lawrence-Bullard. "I fell in love with it, even with its seventies-era shag carpet, mirrors everywhere, and gen-

DREAM WEAVER *Opposite*
Martyn Lawrence-Bullard's
ebonized Anglo-Indian bed
is draped with nineteenth-
century paisleys found in
Paris and London. Also making walk-on appearances are
pieces from his collection
of 1795 English engravings
depicting scenes from
Shakespeare, part of a complete set. The pillows are
custom-cut silk *devore* in
patterns inspired by the
antique paisleys. The lamps
painted coral colors were
from the estate of Tony
Duquette. Antique Louis
Vuitton and Hèrmes trunks
are part of his life long
collection.

eral tackiness."

Lawrence-Bullard cleared the decks and brought in his seventeenth-century Flemish tapestry and topped it with a sixteenth-century Dutch convex mirror, layering on Tony Duquette estate treasures and a tangle of antique Indian whale-oil lanterns.

A French leather sofa from the Marché Paul Bert is lavished with pillows made from an eighteenth-century Portuguese cardinal's robe, stitched with gold and silver thread.

A pair of George IV chairs covered in brown alligator are accompanied by nineteenth-century French gilded footstools with Aubusson tapestry seats bordered in suede. It's lavish and old-world, but somehow, in his hands, lighthearted, irreverent, and madcap at the same time.

The walls of the small (almost nonexistent) kitchen were covered in Zuber "Bibliotheque" paper, to give the impression of a library. The room was previously Norma Talmadge's boudoir.

And how exactly did the former thespian segue from acting to decorating?

"Throughout my years at acting school, I supported myself buying and selling antiques at flea markets in London," said Lawrence-Bullard. "My father was an opera singer, a tenor, so we traveled the world and I saw the best architecture and the most significant, influential interiors. That was my design education."

His first client was Cheryl Tiegs, for whom he dreamed up a Balinese pavilion, and William H. Macy, Lucy Dahl, and Edward Norton soon followed.

As he dashed up Coldwater Canyon for a client meeting, Lawrence-Bullard could not be happier.

"It has been a marvelous cocktail," said the designer. "All of the ingredients have been the most delicious concoction."

THE CRICKET SINGS *Right, and left* Interior designer Michael DePerno's idyllic living room is home to his beloved terrier/whippet, Niki, and her whippet companion, Sticks, who are welcome to snooze on any soft surface of the house. Their *chaise-longue*, covered in blue and beige linen from Diamond Foam and Fabric, was a lucky find at the Porte de Vanves flea market, Paris. A six-foot tall Korean *tansu*, c 1860, was crafted of burled wood, with ornate locks, hinges, and handles of engraved pewter.

VEILS OF MORNING *Following pages* For his light-filled living room, Michael DePerno has gathered an international coterie of art, objects and furniture that live in harmony. The sofa, from DePerno's own collection, REN, is simply detailed in a silk/linen tweed, and stands on a Chinese-style carved and lacquered leg. The travertine-topped table by Paul McCobb was a trophy from the Pasadena Rose Bowl flea market.

ISLAND OF CALM

INTERIOR DESIGNER MICHAEL DEPERNO LIVES IN GREAT COMFORT AND POLISHED STYLE—WITH TWO ELEGANT CANINE COMPANIONS

Los Angeles designer Michael DePerno spent six months living in Stockholm a few years ago. Voyaging out to the archipelago in summer, enjoying the calm, monochromatic landscapes, and reveling in the diffused light, he learned to love the subtle Swedish sense of color, and the traditional Swedish love of nature and natural materials.

DePerno is now living in West Hollywood, and, perhaps almost subliminally, he brings some of the same Swedish appreciation of understatement, simplicity, and paled-down colors to his shingled cottage.

Colors he selected—pale blue, indigo, stone, cream, and soft dove gray—look as if they come from a nineteenth-century Swedish watercolor of remote islands. They confer on his rooms a quiet, harmonious vibe that feels more centered in rural Sonoma County, where he has a country cottage, than the beating heart of Los Angeles.

His rooms are like a tree house, with soft dappled light. From his windows mauve-flowered Jacarandas and fragrant Pittosporum trees come into view.

"I've gathered around me a collection of things that inspire me—that's what my world's about," said DePerno, who also spent time in Manhattan. "I'm always looking for thoughtful placement, well-considered furniture that's simple and beautiful, and a sense of grace."

EVENING FULL OF THE LINNET'S WINGS
Opposite, and left For his bedroom perch, designer Michael DePerno keeps décor cool and calm so that he can hear the birds singing in the evergreen elms in his garden. The platform bed, with a raw silk covered headboard, is from his REN collection. The campaign-style desk and the English slat-back chair were auction finds, in New York. The chair seat is covered with camel-colored cashmere. DePereno furnished his bathroom with a nineteenth-century Chinese rosewood table with a marble top.

DePerno said that in his work as a designer of interiors and furniture, and in his own house, he sees design as a process of layering, adding, editing, changing and simplifying.

"It's inevitable that my room décor will change and flow," he said. "I brought many things from New York, and I've found great objects in Los Angeles, but my country life is now influencing my Los Angeles life, and I enjoy things to be more low-key."

Nature is a constant inspiration.

"I like to be surrounded by pieces of nature—leaves, twigs, shells, baskets woven from reeds, marble, stone, as well as pure fabrics like natural linen, raw silk and soft cotton," said the designer. His floors are oak, stripped and sanded to a satin finish with a soft gray stain and ebony wash.

"The effect I wanted on the floor was the depth and richness of driftwood," said DePerno, who grew up in Michigan. His blue and white porcelain collection and an antique Chinese rug were the inspiration for indigo-dyed pillows.

DePerno finally achieved the serene feeling he wanted in his house.

"Everything is in its place, but my dogs are allowed on everything," he said. "They love soft, cushy places to sleep on. They'll even drag a sweater or a pillow onto the sofa to make it more comfortable, to have a piece of me next to them. Even when they rearrange things, the decorating stays intact. The framework is there—and both the dogs and I are very happy."

ARISTOCRATIC ARCHITECTURE
Below, opposite, and following pages
The house was originally designed in
the early thirties by architect James
Dolena. One of the first decorators
was T. H. Robsjohn-Gibbings. The
house had great bones, said designer
Michael Smith, who gave the rooms
contemporary polish and elegance
with Chippendale armchairs
upholstered in Claremont's striped
silk, an eighteenth-century Swedish
chandelier, and dramatic curtains of
Lemon Ice and Imperial Yellow silk
by Prima Seta. An antique stone
statue graces the three-acre garden
which frames an elegant pool and
distant views of the Pacific Ocean.

THE SOFT GLEAM OF GOLD

WITH ANTIQUES, MICHAEL SMITH FOCUSES ON THE ROMANTIC IDEA OF INDIVIDUALITY, CHARACTER, AND PURE CHARM

In a fast dozen years, Michael Smith has become the decorator of choice for style-conscious Hollywood producers, financiers, directors and stars.

Sleuthing in Celebrityland, it's possible to discover that Smith's A-list clients include Rupert Murdoch, Michelle Pfeiffer, Cindy Crawford, as well as a best-selling novelist, film directors, a fragrance and fashion mogul, a Manhattan surgeon, and top entertainment corporation heads. For one author/producer, he has now polished several houses; for a major box-office star/activist and his wife he is working on houses in California and New York. But you won't hear that from Smith. He's focused on his work, putting together highly individual interiors that paint portraits of his clients. He's looking for antiques.

Smith is admired for the way he uses antiques in an unpre-

tentious way.

"My work has tended to be less formal because of the history of Los Angeles and the way people live here," said Smith. "No one wants intimidating furniture that's stiff and starchy. They want to be able to use rooms, to relax and entertain there."

When asked, he can fashion rooms with a grand, formal look and make them very inviting.

"It's important to realize that eighteenth-century French furniture can be comfortable and not at all uptight," said Smith. "Used in a carefully edited room that is contemporary in feeling, Louis XVI or Chippendale chairs can be light, with great purity of line. They need not look pretentious."

Smith said that to create rooms in a truly personal style—with or without a designer or architect—takes a great deal of trial and error.

"Buying antiques of whatever style or period you favor gives you an opportunity to experiment," noted Smith, who visits the venerated antiques shows in Paris, London and New York to find treasures for his clients.

"Since most people have trouble envisioning custom-made furniture, antiques give you the advantage of offering no surprises," Smith said. "You can buy an antique table, bring it home and live with it and get to know it. Antiques are the pieces you keep."

Smith insists that the days of buying a to-the-teeth "country squire" look or a misguided "French chateau" look for a Santa Monica, Bel Air or Beverly Hills house are truly over.

"Your house must to be relevant to the reality of your life," said the designer. "Decorators have often been the worst perpetrators of a "look" foisted on a client. I consider it unprofessional and boring to design by rote."

Houses should not be theatrical or showy unless that's what you truly are, he said.

"Formal English manor-style or to-the-nines London townhouse look-alike rooms in the Hollywood Hills are probably inappropriate and possibly laughable," he noted.

Most people don't realize that traditional rooms cry out for the contrast of smoothly reductive antiques and twentieth-century pieces to give them an edge. Equally, cool contemporary rooms demand the richness, heft and surprise of well-crafted antiques.

Smith himself has lived in various houses with a handsome Anglo-Dutch sideboard in an all-white bedroom, an eighteenth-century Portuguese table in an Hermès orange study, with a turquoise silk-upholstered sofa and silver-leaf Anglo-Indian tables, and a superglam Regency sofa upholstered in the original brown leather flanked by a pair of steel and plywood Eames bookcases from the fifties.

"I bought the antiques, as I did the modern pieces, for their line and integrity," he said. "Only after I bought them did I think of putting them together. They will also work later in other houses, other rooms. I expect my antiques to have longevity."

Smith haunts Los Angeles antique shops for his clients and has an extraordinary eye for unusual antiques with charm and presence. He avoids the obvious "trophy" antiques, those overly gilded baroque chairs and grandiose rococo sofas that look as if they belong on a stage set, not in a house.

Buying for status is not something he or his clients are interested in.

"I think people are often surprised to discover that I use low-key antiques a lot," said Smith. "The general perception of Hollywood is that stars live in rooms that look like high-style movie sets. Nothing could be fur-

WAKE-UP CALL *Left*
Designer Michael Smith
enhanced the classic English
country house feeling of the
bedroom with Montaigne linen
fabric by Cowtan & Tout on the
walls, extended up into the
ceiling to add height. The bed,
custom-made by Sotheby's
Restoration, was given a jolt of
color with an antique silk quilt,
and draped in blue-gray silk with
a cream and sage green silk
lining. The television is concealed
at the foot of the bed in a
custom-made chinoiserie chest.

the from the truth. They want their houses to be personal, comfortable, and above all individual. Carefully chosen, quality antiques give their rooms character."

For one of his first clients, Smith designed a family house that is both stylish and comfortable. Colors are subtle, memorabilia and art are well displayed.

"Young Hollywood no longer wants rooms that are larger than life," said Smith who tells his new clients that antiques are not solely for novelty. Nor are they just for traditional rooms.

"Antiques bring so much to a room and work with everything," Smith said. "It's never the pair of eighteenth-century French chairs you sell when you move. They're yours for life. You don't tire of your beloved English writing table. They only get better over the years."

"I encourage people to be brave and think of antiques in their own way," said Smith, who, as a major purchaser of antiques for his clients is greeted very warmly in antique emporiums of Los Angeles, New York and Paris.

Antiques are more versatile than brand new furniture. Nicks and chips and signs of loving use and wear only confer more character.

"An antique mahogany tea table can be used as a bedside table, an end table, or a lamp table," he said. "To me, a new coffee table is just a coffee table."

Smith said that some people are afraid to start collecting antiques because they are puzzled by their mystique. Antique shops can be intimidating.

"An entire shop filled with antiques can be daunting," he admitted. "In the store that scholarly approach and seriousness are appropriate. That doesn't mean you have to aim for museum-like authenticity. It's best to mix periods in your own rooms—give antiques your own spin and don't limit your choices."

"For my younger clients, I suggest they start with perhaps a pair of chairs," he said. "I always go looking for antiques with a sense of curiosity. You may search for a mahogany sideboard and find instead a smashing Flemish painted chest. Always be open-minded."

Smith never tires of walking into antique shops and auction houses—in Antwerp, Venice, Santa Barbara, or San Francisco.

"Collecting antiques should always be done in the most optimistic way," said Smith. "Buy the best you can afford—and enjoy your favorite pieces every day."

LEAVES OF GRASS *Below* The Stamps house in South Pasadena is hidden behind Kate and Odom's romantic plantings of old roses, lilies, ferns, lavender, hellebores and euphorbia. The family lives a charmed life in their house beneath one-hundred-year-old carob trees, purple wisteria, pittosporum, and fragrant orange trees.

COUNTRY AIR *Opposite* Odom Stamps polished and shaped the interior architecture of the living room, adding a new fireplace and paneling the walls and the ceiling with pine planks with a pale glaze. A late eighteenth-century Irish boxwood mantel makes a perfect perch for flowers from the Stamps garden. "Old Rose" chintz, John Fowler's favorite pattern, covers a Regency-style armchair and an oval-back Louis XVI-style fauteuil. An eighteenth-century English mahogany serpentine chest, and a down-filled sofa from New Orleans, are framed with antique Scottish paisley shawls used as curtains.

PASADENA PERSPECTIVE
KATE AND ODOM STAMPS RESCUED AN HISTORIC CARRIAGE-HOUSE AND ALLOWED ITS SPIRIT TO SOAR

One hot summer day, a handful of years ago, Kate and Emma Stamps made a magical discovery.

Under the spell of a for sale sign hanging askew on a fence in a leafy enclave near the Arroyo Seco in South Pasadena, they wandered down a weed-choked garden path.

"We saw this bedraggled one-bedroom cottage with a sleeping porch, surrounded by a completely private garden," recalled Kate, a noted interior designer.

She returned early the next morning with her husband Odom, an architect who is also the mayor *pro tem* of South Pasadena.

"It was like a romantic house in the woods—totally enchanting but not at all practical for a family of three," said Kate. "We

A PASSION FOR PAINTINGS
Opposite A life-long collection of eighteenth-century English, Dutch, Flemish, Italian and English watercolors found on travels to Europe are gathered in the sitting room above a luxurious brown velvet sofa found on the sidewalk on La Brea Avenue in Los Angeles. The gilded obelisk is eighteenth-century Venetian.

INVITATION TO DINE *Left*
Seven layers of persimmon-colored glaze give the pine-paneled dining room a delicious glow. The Georgian-style corner cabinet was made by George von Wahlde, Kate's father, who is a master craftsman. A Soumac flat-weave rug covers the table. "We love to entertain, so once a week we jam eight or ten guests around our dining table, and it's great fun," said Kate. "We use every antique—our port glasses, Wedgewood tureens, silver serving platters and chargers, Georgian glass bowls, and for a final flourish, Swedish turquoise enamel *demi-tasse* spoons."

immediately bought it."

The house, they learned, had been built in 1904 as a carriage house for a grand mansion (no longer standing). Horse-drawn carriages were sheltered beneath the structure, and the chauffeur's quarters were above.

"Our plan from the start was to reconfigure the house and make functional improvements but keep the unpretentious style intact," said Odom, whose family has a long history in art and antiques in New Orleans.

He enclosed the former flimsy sleeping porch and wrapped it with a white-painted balustrade to suggest its former use. South Pasadena (like most of California) is earthquake country, so the house was buttressed and supported on a steel moment frame concealed in stone piers, crafted with local arroyo stones.

The enclosed porch is now a dining room and sit-

ting room. Two bedrooms were artfully carved out of one, with a romantic built-in sleeping alcove. Storage is concealed below beds and behind carved panels.

Beneath the house, where the carriages were parked in its earlier life, there is now a sheltered porch were the family keeps exercise equipment, a garden swing, and a table and chairs for weekend lunches.

Pine boards with a pale translucent glaze were installed on the living room walls and ceiling. And out came the Stamps & Stamps lifetime collections of paintings, Flemish tapestries, Turkish rugs, English creamware, Regency chairs, rare silver and crystal, and family heirlooms.

"We didn't want the house to look too done or too decorated," said Kate, "I've got a bit of an anti-decoration streak and here we wanted to turn down the volume,

READING GROUP *Right* A Clarence House toile depicting neoclassical scenes covers a favorite armchair in the entrance hall. A late eighteenth-century chest-on-chest in plum pudding mahogany, and built-in shelves which hold their extensive collections of gardening and design books, give a sense of architecture and structure to the small room. The painted walls are a Stamps & Stamps concoction of custom-mixed green-gray.

SENSE AND SENSIBILITY *Opposite* Emma Stamps's bedroom looks as if it leapt from the pages of Jane Austen. A French-inspired toile by Colefax & Fowler covers the antique French headboard, which is draped in undyed silk broadcloth.

and loosen up the look. We used some "off" and odd colors, like gray-green or faded rose, and some almost clashing colors like several shades of blue together."

Faithful to the original structure, Odom worked to enhance the barn-like quality of the cottage. The living room ceiling was opened up to the attic to maximize the height and size of the room.

Their house, with its faded English chintzes and old Turkish rugs, welcomes two rambunctious dogs. A gray Weimaraner called Bubba, and Spare, a Golden retriever/huskie mix, are the beloved companions of Emma, an arts history student.

"It's now a very comfortable house," said Kate, who is originally from Michigan. "Friends from New Orleans think it looks very English. And our English chums think it has a French style. We're total Anglophiles, but

we also have a great fondness for Gustavian neoclassical furniture, Middle Eastern textiles, French toiles, Craftsman architecture, Gothic pieces, Italian baroque, Moroccan colors and rugs. And we've filled the garden with two thousand David Austin roses."

On summer evenings, the garden is like a perfumery.

"We swoon from the night-blooming jasmine," said Kate. "This is an entrancing place. When we come home, we leave our cares behind."

THROWING A CURVE *Right*

For the thirties-inspired living room of
his Streamline Moderne house in the
Hollywood Hills, Michael Berman
favors colors like taupe, celadon,
butterscotch, and cream. The low-key
colors are a pefect foil for the
ebonized silhouettes of his chairs and
the glamorous mirrored coffee table.
Increasing the glamour quotient here:
The Berman-designed tall "JMF" lamp,
his "Tamarind" sofa and striped
"Warner" club chairs, for Michael
Berman Limited, through design
showrooms. At right, is a vintage Paul
Frankl chair. The screen was salvaged
from the late, lamented Bullock's
Wilshire store. Rush matting and
simple woodwork keep the
thirties homage firmly anchored
in the present.

A SPIRIT OF OPTIMISM

INTERIOR DESIGNER MICHAEL BERMAN APPRECIATES THE SOFT CURVES AND WARM HUMANISM OF THIRTIES STREAMLINE MODERNE

Michael Berman seldom wavers from the beautifully controlled,
elegantly retro style he has polished and honed over the last two
decades. He lists as one of his design inspirations the highly
intellectual, sculptural work of San Francisco's revered interiors
and furniture designer, John Dickinson.

"I admired the way John Dickinson edited his rooms, paring
them down to essentials," said Berman. "I try to keep that same
control in my own rooms."

Thirties Streamline Moderne architecture and interiors are
one of Berman's passions. This distinctly American style was a
reaction to the fussiness and frou-frou of throwing Victorian and
Edwardian aesthetic. Influenced by aerodynamic auto designs, and
the sleek silhouettes of transatlantic liners, and nudged by the
more rigorous philosophy of the Bauhaus, Streamline Moderne

FOR YOUR DINING PLEASURE
Previous spread A bleached oak "Compass" table by Donghia was a gift from Angelo Donghia. The "Petite Klismos" chairs covered in chamois-colored wool burlap are from the Michael Berman Limited collection of furniture and accessories. A Bauer pottery urn from the forties is piled with bougainvillea. In the intense light of Los Angeles, every degree of color matters, so the designer modulates his color palette for daytime and nighttime effect.

SWEET SLUMBER *Opposite, and right* Berman is a committed editor of his own designs, and seldom likes the present to intrude too much into his homage to thirties style and optimism. Electronics are concealed in a cabinet. The bedroom, which overlooks the garden, has Steamline Moderne plaster detailing around the walls and a neatly tailored headboard. Colors are muted, pattern is banished. The whirlpool bath, neatly wedged into a corner.

architects embellished buildings with portholes, curved walls and overhangs, scrolls and Art Deco motifs, and the modern statement of steel-framed windows.

Interiors of Steamline Moderne houses were glamorized with plaster "ziggurats," fluted Deco-style chair railings, curvy stair balustrades, and of-the-period plaster goddesses.

"Streamline Moderne defined progress and suggested a more optimistic, glamorous modernism," noted Berman. "It was simple, clean, and restrained. It still looks modern."

Berman's own house, in Bronson Canyon in the Hollywood Hills just below the "Hollywood" sign, looks like a thirties ocean liner, with porthole windows, and a front terrace curved like the prow of a ship, complete with ship's railing.

Berman found it by chance a decade ago, and after a quick burst of remodeling, he painted the walls shades of green/taupe sharkskin, espresso bean, and pale taupe outlined with Slipper White by Farrow & Ball.

"My color schemes relate to the tones that were in vogue in Hollywood in the thirties," said Berman, who shares the house with his longtime partner, Lee Weinstein, a psychotherapist. "I love colors that have some ambiguity."

Berman has a particular fondness for certain muted browns, soft greens, a chartreuse with bite, dreamy purple/eggplant, and soothing grays, all outlined with just-back-from-the-laundry white and a slightly tinted ecru.

"I choose colors that are paled-down rather than shocking," noted Berman. "I like to work with colors I can live with for a long time."

The fabrics he selects tend to be smooth and sensuous, a soothing wrap for his shapely furniture.

Ribbed cotton chenille with thick bullion cording, natural canvas, silk velvet, taffeta and vintage woven textiles are among his favorites.

"I like a look that is reminiscent of the glamorous Golden Age, but updated, not a slavish copy," said Berman. "I'm not creating a period piece, but rather bringing together found original pieces with designs from my own furniture collection."

It's glamour without the glitz or hard edge. Berman said he is a scavenger by nature and mixes periods and styles.

"The luxury and comfort are inspired by the movies of the thirties, but it's restrained, less fussy, and less ornamented," said the designer. "This is not the old idea of glamour."

Berman, like other Los Angeles designers, thinks that rooms come alive when old and new, lavish and not-so, intermingle. He may spend $75 on a dining chair, or $500 on a piece of studio pottery if it moves him. He uses vintage and contemporary photography in his rooms.

"This house has been a great place for me to test prototypes of my new designs and I am completely at home in this neighborhood," said Berman. "Bronson Canyon is like a village, with cafes and art galleries. It's an oasis far from the fast pace of Sunset Boulevard. We have raccoons and deer walking up to the door, but in five minutes we can be having dinner at Musso & Frank's on Hollywood Boulevard. Griffith Park is close by. I wouldn't want to live anywhere else in Los Angeles."

ATTENTION TO DETAIL
A second-century Roman mosaic fragment, fashioned by Madeline Stuart into a table with a hand-forged iron base, stands on an antique Oushak carpet from Aga John. A pair of Italian velvet-wrapped iron *torcheres* with Fortuny shades frame the new fireplace. Jean Horihata gilded and painted the new plaster ceiling cove. The sofa, designed by Stuart, is dressed in a custom tea-dyed damask, and pillows of *strié* silk velvet and vintage Fortuny fabric. The chair is covered in a gauffraged linen velvet by Scalamandré. Beyond the sitting room is the bedroom.

SLEEPING BEAUTY

DESIGNER MADELINE STUART CRAFTS SUITE REPOSE
FOR PRODUCER GALE ANN HURD AND
SCREENWRITER/DIRECTOR JONATHAN HENSLEIGH

Like a sentinel from another century, the house of Gale Ann Hurd and Jonathan Hensleigh stands high above an arroyo near Pasadena.

Originally built in 1925 by Sylvanus Marston, the quintessential Pasadena-area architect, their twenty-room house features Grand Tour Mediterranean-inspired architecture, superbly detailed down to the last door pull.

As a film producer, Gale Ann Hurd numbers the *Terminator* series, *Armageddon*, and the *Alien* series among her credits. Jonathan Hensleigh is a noted screenwriter, director, and producer, whose film credits include *The Punisher*, and *Die Hard with a Vengeance*.

"It's an absolutely spectacular house," said Los Angeles designer Madeline Stuart. "Every architectural gesture is well-expressed and beautifully proportioned. The original owners and their architect traveled throughout Spain and Italy to find architectural details to enrich the house."

Baroque iron balconies, handcrafted sconces, twelfth-century Spanish floor tiles, carved ceilings, and carved and gild-

VISIONS OF VELÀSQUEZ *Opposite, and right* The four-poster bed, designed by Madeline Stuart, was inspired by an eighteenth-century Spanish bed she saw in a painting in the Prado. The bronze silk bed canopy, which has a beaded trim by M & J Trimming in New York City, hovers above a Scalamandré silk damask bed cover. The etching is by Joan Miró. The television trunk, with handcarved and gilded lion's-paw feet, is upholstered in acid green silk velvet. It's a Madeline Stuart design. The *chaise-longue* is covered in silk velvet, and the bedside tables are nineteenth-century Anglo-Indian. The rug of wool and silk was crafted in Nepal by Tibetan weavers.

twelfth-century door frames from a Spanish monastery enhance the time-out-of-time feeling.

"There's a great luxurious devotion to detail throughout the house, and it was a pleasure to work there," said Stuart. "It's now a refuge that respects and acknowledges the history of this magnificent place."

In designing the master bedroom suite, a former rabbit warren of tiny rooms which had been further desecrated with ersatz Tuscan décor, Stuart first took the series of rooms and an outdoor terrace down to the studs.

"I wanted to clarify and clean up the floor plan, and to create a sense of coherence and luxury," said the designer. "My goal was to design a world that expressed the colors, textures, and sensibilities of earlier centuries with fine craftsmanship and artistry."

Stuart's new plan for the suite included a spacious sitting room, a large bedroom with a its own enclosed terrace, and a pair of dramatic new bathrooms.

"I selected custom-dyed silk velvets, tea-dyed damasks, and handmade antique carpets, and designed tiles that looked as if they had been part of the house

for decades," Stuart said. "Furniture, lighting, art, and mirrors were selected so that they appear to have been found over many years. It's the antithesis of a room that betrays instant decorating. I rail against rooms that look brand new or as if everything arrived on a truck on the same day."

Stuart's colors evoke paintings by Velàsquez, Turner in Venice, and the muddy reds and bronzy greens of seventeenth-century Spain.

"Some of the luxury is tactile," said the designer. "The curtains are heavy velvet, the rails are hand-forged iron, pillows are silk velvet, the carpet is silk and wool. I was interpreting a European idiom but keeping the references somewhat light-hearted. This is California, after all, so the allusions are subtle, lightly suggested."

Stuart's client was moved to tears when she first saw the completed rooms. "I took that as an enormous compliment," said Stuart.

CALM AND COLLECTED In the entry hall, the floor is terra cotta pavers with a French limestone border. A pair of Louis XIV folding garden benches of wood and leather, signed Jacob, were de-accessioned from the Louvre collections. The late eighteenth-century French stone-topped table was also found in Paris. The antique white marble urns are French, in the Greek style. They are placed on marble plinths. In the sitting room, Fernandez has placed an eighteenth-century French limestone fireplace, and a nineteenth-century Italian mirror that belonged to beauty mogul Helena Rubenstein in the thirties. The pair of nineteenth-century Italian mahogany chairs are of no particular provenance, said Fernandez, but he liked the straightforward silhouette. The walls are plaster.

CLASSIC WALDO

IN A BEVERLY HILLS ENCLAVE, WALDO FERNANDEZ REFINES, EDITS, AND PERFECTS HIS PARED-DOWN INTERIORS

Designers in Los Angeles do, indeed, live like their high-profile clients. Some live with even greater style than their clients.

Fourteen-years ago, interior designer Waldo Fernandez—he's usually called simply "Waldo"—built himself a house on Sunset Boulevard in Beverly Hills that is mogul-sized, and filled with Greek statuary, Roman marble torsos, and English antiques.

"This was my fantasy of how I wanted to live," said Fernandez.

Clients over the years have included Elizabeth Taylor (the godmother of his son), Burt Bacharach, Sean Connery, Michael York, Brad Pitt…and Jennifer Aniston, and now Tobey McGuire.

"For my clients, I am flexible and I work in a range of styles," said Fernandez. "For myself, I am perhaps more experimental, more rigorous. My house is, in effect, a laboratory."

His residence is conveniently located near the Beverly Hills Hotel.

"I bought the lot I loved, and it had a not very distinguished house on it, so I took it down to the foundation and started from zero," he said.

For the U-shaped house, which surrounds a pool and paved terrace, Fernandez designed plain plaster and parchment walls, and terra-cotta paver floors with a grid framing of French limestone. He prefers consistent materials to make the transitions from room to room more harmonious.

"The house was new, but because of my Cuban background I wanted it to have a feeling of age, to have soul," said the designer. "I chose materials, like marble and terra-cotta, brick and plaster, which show subtle signs of age and wear, which improve over time. I love massive scale, so the room volumes are large, with lots of light. I have tall French doors which open to the garden, and several rooms have skylights. I fill the rooms with greens and plants, and that's very L.A."

SPARKLING DIALOGUE The study is Fernandez's tribute to Jacques-Émile Ruhlmann and chic Paris taste of the thirties and forties, his newest passion. A pair of Ruhlmann chairs, covered in taupe suede, and a Jacques Adnet sofa and chairs covered in dark green taffeta, give the room heft and comfort. Collections of second century BC Roman busts and marble fragments stand on the console table. The wall is covered in faux parchment. The floor is terra-cotta pavers with a frame of French limestone.

The exterior of the house is brick with a whitewash. Twenty-foot-tall ficus hedges shelter the house on all four sides. A pair of massive wooden gates painted dark taupe/brown are the only sign that a high-profile designer lives within.

"I'm fanatical about keeping everything in perfect order," said Fernandez. "I have the gates painted every few months, and the hedges are clipped using a plumb line and string to get them absolutely perfectly straight. It has to be done by hand—none of those machines which chop and churn up the branches."

Fernandez left his native Cuba in the sixties with his family, alighted briefly in New York, and got his start in design working on sets and décor on the Fox lot. After director John Schlesinger hired him to design the interiors for his house, the Fernandez design firm and an antiques gallery were launched.

"My design has evolved over the years, but antiques of various periods have been a constant," said Fernandez. "When I'm making a change, trying a transition from one style to another, I put a room together of the elements I like as a bit of an experiment. I see how it works, check the silhouettes, watch how materials work together."

He experimented in the study, where he has retained his favorite Greek and Roman marble and terra-cotta sculptures

MONASTIC LUXURY *Opposite* Fernandez appreciates subtle, up-close luxury that does not shriek. His headboard is upholstered in eggshell-colored silk velvet that was hand-embroidered in India. The bed-skirt is made of the same fabric. A pair of late seventeenth century Italian painted tables frame the bed. An antique Chinese cabinet with lacquered doors, found in Paris, conceals the television and electronics.

BALANCE AND ORDER *Below* In a sitting room beside the bedroom, Fernandez has composed a dramatic vignette with a German neoclassical *secretaire* by Roentgen in crutch mahogany with bronze inlay, Robert Mapplethorpe photographs, from 1988, and an Italian neoclassical chair. Also in the room is an eighteenth-century English chair with elaborate carving that he vows never to sell.

from earlier days, but he has now introduced Jacques Adnet, Jacques-Émile Ruhlmann, and Jean-Michel Frank originals and pieces in the manner of Paris salon furniture, to test the waters.

"I'm in the process of building a new house, higher up in Beverly Hills, and now I'm seriously collecting twentieth-century classic French furniture from the thirties and forties by Rateau, Adnet, Jean-Michel Frank, and Ruhlmann," said Fernandez, who founded a design firm to produce reproduction furniture, in addition to running his own interior design company. "I'm thinking of de-accessioning many of my more serious English and Italian antiques."

The study illustrates the designer's current transition from his previous décor using serious antiques, rich gilding, ormolu, marble and the classic European traditions he admired for three decades, to a twentieth-century modern approach, even a nod to modernism.

A pair of club chairs upholstered in taupe suede, designed by Jacques-Émile Ruhlmann, accompany a sofa and chairs designed by Adnet.

GRACE AND FAVOR *Left, and below* A Greek marble statue that Fernandez found in the South of France holds court near the swimming pool. "I fell in love with her face, the proportions, the fine carving," said the designer. "I had to have it. Now I can see the statue from almost every room of the house and I enjoy it every day, plus its reflection in the pool. I'm never selling that." The terrace can be enjoyed most of the year. The eleven-foot, six-inch-tall doors have gold-plated French hardware. "They're like Giacometti, but gold-plated," noted Fernandez. "They're polished every day, and they're really shiny, really beautiful."

The Greek marble vases, terra-cotta sculpture fragments, and Roman archaeological dig finds he has been collecting for decades probably won't make the cut. Nor will the elegant Louis XIV folding garden chairs of leather and wood, with the Jacob stamp, or his baroque Italian marble-topped console tables that made such a handsome stage for marble busts and torsos.

The glamour will still be there in his next house, along with the perfectly pruned hedges. But he's unsentimental about editing out the eighteenth century and embracing the twentieth. For Waldo's next design statement it's definitely bye-bye Louis, and hello Jean-Michel.

OVER-ARCHING In earlier, innocent decades, guests wandered in to the Chateau Marmont through this grand Gothic colonnade, fashioned after the architecture of one Loire Valley chateau or another. Now guests can sip tea or a twilight Campari here, then stroll to the bar and the restaurant nearby. Oh, and by the way. It's pronounced Marmont, to the very last t. The Chateau Marmont is situated on Marmont Lane which was named for the English silent movie actor, Percy Marmont. Ongoing renovations by hotelier André Balazs have removed a layer of shabbiness but kept its bohemian air.

CHAPTER 5
GLAMOUR ESCAPES

HOLLYWOOD HAS SOME OF THE MOST SEDUCTIVE HOTELS IN THE WORLD. WITH THEIR PALM-SHADED SWIMMING POOLS, HOTHOUSE FLOWERS, PRIVATE ENTRANCES, CHOREOGRAPHED VALET PARKING, LUXURIOUS GARDEN BUNGALOWS AND THE HOPE OF A CELEBRITY ENCOUNTER, THEY OFFER ENTERTAINMENT, ESCAPISM, AND LUSTY GRATIFICATION FOR THE EGO.

It's a typical afternoon at the Hotel Bel-Air swimming pool. An Oscar-winning screenwriter is reading the *New Yorker* in one corner, a blonde starlet in a tiny bikini sleeps in the sun with occasional sips of Perrier, and no one pays attention to one of the sexiest stars alive who wanders on and off stage in his plush robe, then settles to read the *New York Times*. Over at the Chateau Marmont, there's a script conference in the colonnade, and that hot new director (who? who?) straggles in from his trans-Pacific flight. Maison 140's Bar Noir is a little bit of Paris in Beverly Hills. It's all very low-key at these hotels, even when a famous star arrives for her baby shower, or Oprah gives a dinner party for fifty of her famous friends. Jasmine scents the air, caviar and Champagne are just a phone call away. At the Viceroy, there are ocean views and Alice-in-Wonderland *chaises-longues* with curves for days. Life could be this good.

CHATEAU COOL

THE CHATEAU MARMONT IS THE FAVORITE HANGOUT
FOR HOLLYWOOD'S CREATIVES. FORTUNATE
INDEED ARE THOSE WITH A CONTRACT, A CHECK,
AND MONTHS AT THE MARMONT

Jay McInerney wrote the first draft of his first screenplay there.

The Chateau Marmont, he said, "seemed very far away from the Hollywood dealmaking machinery and the wide-eyed, love-you-babe *bonhomie*." He flew in from New York, checked in, and received a phone call from his new agent beside the pool. He'd arrived. And he loved the "international boho atmosphere".

Dennis Hopper, bare-chested, posed with Christopher Walken for Annie Leibovitz in one of the hillside bungalows. Dominick Dunne covered famous trials from there in his paper-strewn room. For years Helmut and June Newton spent winters in "their" penthouse to escape the chill of Monaco. Helmut photographed one of his Domestic Nudes in the Chateau Marmont laundry room. Errol Flynn entertained lolitas. Bruce Weber photographed models. Bill Cosby posed for photographer Dennis Hopper.

Every one, it seems, ends up, sooner or later, posing at the Chateau Marmont.

Led Zeppelin drove their Harleys through the lobby. Greta Garbo hid, the Rolling Stones rocked, Carole Lynley flirted. John Belushi checked out. And the cast list continues: Raquel Welch, Gore Vidal, Anna Magnani, Marilyn Monroe, Marlon Brando, Ethan Hawke, Moby, Björk, and Spike Jonze all stayed there, though not in the same room.

Sylvia Sydney lived there for years with her tiny dog, and could often be seen in the afternoon, like Gloria Swanson's ghost, strolling along the colonnade dressed in a suit, with a hat perched just so.

The history of the Chateau Marmont is the history of Hollywood.

It started life ambitiously in 1929 as a very grand apartment building. Theatrically modeled after a Norman chateau, it was Loire Valley meets Sunset Boulevard.

The Chateau Marmont, standing majestically on Marmont Avenue, was advertised as "the first earthquake-proof building in Los Angeles, constructed without regard to expense." Two years later, the Chateau Marmont was relaunched as a hotel.

The apartments became suites and rooms. They're spacious, comfortable, and equipped with kitchens and white-hot views of Los Angeles and West Hollywood. Rooms feel more like home than a hotel, and that suits

COOL AND THEN SOME
Right, and below
The drawing room at the
Chateau Marmont looks
today almost exactly the
way it has looked for
decades. There's the same
terra-cotta floor, and the
same furniture, now
refreshed and spiffed up but
in the same style, the same
noncorporate manner, the
retro mood. Some guests,
incognito, dash through,
while others, longing for
companionship or recogni-
tion, linger with a newspaper
or a drink. Someone always
comes along.

guests and residents just fine.

Kenneth Tynan and Kit Carson swore they saw ghosts.
Many guests have "lucky" rooms where they've enjoyed success
of one kind or another.

Rooms at the back, quiet and shadow-dappled, overlook a
residential street. From this perch it's tempting to spy on and
surmise about the neighbors, as writer/longtime resident
Dominick Dunne did in his novel, *Another City, Not My Own*,
much of which takes place at the Chateau Marmont. Dunne
noted that the only time he ever complained to the manager was
when his shirts came back from the laundry on hangers instead
of folded and boxed, as he liked them.

Julian Schnabel might be chatting in the drawing room,
Emilio Estevez arriving with a Playboy Bunny, or Linda
Evangelista sipping Champagne. Leonardo di Caprio, Winona
Ryder, Keanu, and Natalie, they've all been there. Feigning dis-
interest is the only attitude—or nonattitude. To look or even
glance is to appear uncool.

Arriving at the Chateau Marmont is no grand ceremony.
The entry and reception desk are not as pretentious nor impres-

A SPLASH, A DASH *Opposite, and left* The pool is somewhat small and quaint by Hollywood standards, and that's what makes it great. There, Jay McInerney reportedly went looking for a topless sunbather and instead saw Sting bobbing in the pool. The suites—former apartments—include funky kitchens, and breakfast rooms, and inviting, frisky sitting rooms and bedrooms designed by Shawn Hausman, an accomplished Hollywood set designer and event producer. The son of actress Diane Varsi, Hausman has celebrated the essence of cool in his retro rooms at the Marmont, with mid-century modern chairs, boxy sofas, estate-sale art, and vintage lighting, all with a non-decorated air. Hausman has captured the appeal of the Chateau Marmont interiors precisely by seeming not to design, while keeping tight control on the décor. The non-décor décor, that is.

sive as the turrets-and-balconies architecture might suggest, which suits the recluses just fine. John Waters or Daryl Hannah may wander past as bags arrive from the garage. Sofia Coppola and her dad could be coming in for a drink or a script meeting. Still, it's possible on a steamy summer afternoon to linger in the lobby waiting for a bellman and see no one.

Over the last decade or so, the rooms and the drawing room and bar have been updated and refreshed, very slowly and with great care. This may be news to some guests, who imagine that the funky old mohair-covered Chesterfields in the drawing room, and the flea market-esque Frankl chairs and amateur portraits have always belonged to the hotel.

Shawn Hausman, a talented interior designer/set designer/event producer, is responsible for the perfectly cool restorations and invisible rearrangements and updates, performed over time, and unobtrusively.

Hausman has orchestrated the chrome dinette sets in some breakfast rooms, upholstered the Jean-Michel Frank-ish old sofas in off-colors with a retro feeling, and added quirky old lamps and telephone tables that look as if they started life with the hotel's original residents—except they didn't.

Old-timers don't get nervous or disconcerted because it always looks loose yet stylish, and all the suites and rooms have their own odd-ball character. They're inviting, never intimidating.

The Chateau Marmont inspires deep devotion. Billy Wilder said, "I would rather sleep in a bathroom than in any other hotel".

The public rooms—the lobby, the drawing room—

have a vaguely Spanish Colonial feeling, and the chairs and tables look as if they might have been used on a movie set, which they weren't. The décor in the suites is mid-century Americana, with mismatched Noguchi-style coffee tables, Royère-esque floor lamps, and no great sense of the twenty-first century. There's always the notion that Robert de Niro or Drew Barrymore, or someone cooler-than-thou just left.

The Marlboro Man gazes through the window from his sculpted pedestal on a Sunset Boulevard curve.

Every guest has a different reason for loving and lingering at the Marmont. Some come for the suites and stay for the views. Others like the (very) understated service, the slow-to-update telephones and bathrooms. Some adore the roar that rises from Sunset Boulevard on Friday nights, the place to be!

Many guests prefer to relax in the rooms on the hillside-facing north, which are cool and silent and private. Breakfast there, white-bread toast and all, is taken slow, with the *Los Angeles Times* and the trades for entertainment.

"If you must get into trouble, do it at the Chateau Marmont", advised Harry Cohn, to Hollywood hopefuls Glenn Ford and William Holden in 1939.

Things seem a bit quieter these days. Novels are written there, scripts are completed, deals done. When you've stayed there, you've experienced Hollywood. And you'll be back.

WATERS OF DELIGHT *Below*
The oval-shaped swimming pool at the Hotel Bel-Air is sheltered with palm trees in what was formerly the Bel-Air Stables and riding ring. It's all very hush-hush, very discreet, even when famous stars sun themselves on the teak *chaises-longues* and take lunch, or super-hot stars spend the day around the pool reading scripts, and escaping from the paparazzi.

A MISSION TO PLEASE *Opposite*
More than fifteen gardeners, many of whom have been with the Hotel Bel-Air for decades, prune, plant, trim, nurture, plant, and clip the gardens and the rare specimen plants to look as *au naturel* and luxuriant as possible. The Southern California climate blesses the astonishingly lush growth, although it is often very cool and damp in winter.

ELEGANCE PERFECTED

IN RUSTIC STONE CANYON, THE HOTEL BEL-AIR OFFERS LUXURIOUS SUITES, HUSHED PRIVACY, HISTORY, AND RARE DELIGHTS WITHIN A GLAMOROUS GARDEN

To be a guest at the Hotel Bel-Air is to experience bliss. There, all is *ordre, beauté, luxe, calme et volupté*. Walking in the gardens is like entering a voluptuous painting by Henri Matisse. Staying for days or weeks, an indulged guest begins to understand the sensual, romantic poems of Charles Baudelaire.

Arrival is auspicious. After a fast spin through Bel-Air and glimpses of the most closely manicured real estate in the world, a guest enters the hotel's hushed grounds across an arched stone bridge and through the welcoming and winding green arms of noble Western sycamores and stone pine trees. A bell tower wrapped in a red-flowered trumpet vine stands beside delicate tree ferns and extravagant fan palms.

The glittering commerce of Rodeo Drive and Wilshire Boulevard are far away as stone fountains and fragrant Mission-

style courtyards, hummingbirds hovering in a tangle of jasmine, trellised rose gardens, and an oval swimming pool and leafy arbors come into view. At last there's a garden suite with a fire blazing in the fireplace. The only sound is the quiet rustle of palm trees overhead.

A first impulse is never to depart.

The Hotel Bel-Air, which opened in 1946 in a former private estate, is set amid twelve acres of verdant specimen trees, coast redwoods, bird-of-paradise trees, yellow-flowered tipu trees, garden courtyards, and bougainvillea-shaded terraces. The luscious planting creates a hot-house atmosphere that's conducive to red-hot romance, elegant weddings, reclusive retreats, even business meetings.

Guests over the decades have included an international almanac of royalty, along with award-winning actors, heads-of-state, and a glittering roster of celebrities who appreciate and require privacy and superbly discreet service, as well as the highly individual, classic interiors.

The Hotel Bel-Air has written its own rules for low-key, understated luxury. Here it is understood that glitz and flash are not synonymous with delight. Retraint is all.

No two of the ninety-one suites are alike, an attribute that enhances the sense of spending time at a private residence. Some suites have private entrances. Others have quirky circular studies, kitchens, loggias overlooking a quiet hillside, eccentric layouts which include grand stairways, as well as handcrafted iron gates, tiled patios, carved and painted doors, antique lanterns, and one-of-a-kind sitting rooms with hand-painted ceilings.

The Hotel Bel-Air recently redesigned many of the suites. Designer Sybil van Dijs created new suites, under consultation with guests who often stay for several months each year. The result is superbly detailed, somewhat theatrical rooms with a touch of fantasy and the trappings of glamour.

In the Chalon Suite, a custom-painted plaster ceiling reminiscent of elaborate embellishments in Persian palaces mirrors the tracery of the vegetable-dyed Persian rug.

In the Herb Garden Suite, luxurious custom-designed fabrics by F. Schumacher & Co., and Kneedler Fauchere are patterned in classic floral patterns, in soft colors.

So seductive is this velvety hideaway that residents of nearby houses in Stone Canyon often take weekend breaks here, and Italian directors or French stars come to stay for a few days and end up living here for months.

Bellinis are served on the terrace. Earl Grey tea arrives with fresh-baked scones and jam. The sun rises over the glistening palm trees. White wisteria drifts in the gentle breeze.

It's impossible to contemplate departure.

PAGING CEDRIC GIBBONS
Kelly Wearstler's fearless sense of glamour and fun seems to have been inspired by the twenties and thirties films of Cedric Gibbons. The style name used here is Hollywood Regency, a title that would baffle any English designer but which makes perfect sense in a town that takes its movie references seriously. Wearstler's art: deft control of color, a splash of parrot green, and the strength of repetition. Thanks to Wearstler's ineffable style, the Viceroy hotel in Santa Monica (and the new Viceroy in Palm Springs) have been a roaring success.

HOTEL GLAMOUR REVIVAL

DESIGNER KELLY WEARSTLER INFUSED THE VICEROY WITH VERVE, VIVID COLORS, AND A SPLASH OF HOLLYWOOD REGENCY

Parrot green, tobacco brown, sharp lemon, wave-crest white, and silvery driftwood gray are not colors you see every day in a Los Angeles hotel. That's why they appealed to designer Kelly Wearstler, who mined Hollywood's glamorous thirties and forties movie sets, a bit of Billy Haines décor, along with motifs filched from English design history, for the super-glam Viceroy hotel in Santa Monica.

"We started with a rather nondescript hotel building from the sixties, but in the most wonderful location overlooking a stretch of beach," said Wearstler, originally from South Carolina.

Wearstler and Brad Korzen, a real estate developer and hotelier, originally from Chicago, dreamed up a master design and style plan for the proposed hotel, down to the music, the uniforms, and doorknobs, the vibe of the bars, the restaurant menus,

WHAT'S THE DISH *Below*
Kelly Wearstler arranged
more than two hundred and
fifty pieces of English china
of many styles against a
green mirrored wall in the
restaurant of Viceroy

WHITE IS RIGHT *Following
pages* White terry-cloth
covered chairs and *chaises*
give the swimming pool and
terrace a classic Hollywood
feeling. Arquitectonica were
the project's architects.

and the ambiance of the rooms. Korzen and Wearstler are now married.

"The beach is near Los Angeles and in the shadow of Hollywood so I've made it a kind of urban glamour feeling, played up some English design elements, but given it broad gestures that play to today's eclectic design sensibilities," said Wearstler, founder of KWID (Kelly Wearstler Interior Design), her multi-disciplinary firm based in Los Angeles.

"The basic structure was bland, so I planned bold green and crisp white and dark chocolate brown as the glue to hold it all together", noted the designer. English elements, like the exploded architectural motifs on the graphic green, black, and white carpet and a series of niches that display liquor bottles in the bar, have an cleverly ambiguous could-be-seventies-tongue-in-cheek, could-be-Pucci-goes-to-the-movies look.

"I use white against dark brown or green to give the space energy and contrast," said Wearstler, who has also set trends

SHEER EXAGGERATION
Opposite For the Viceroy lobby, Kelly Wearstler designed the Casper wing-back *chaise*, super-size wing-back *chaise-longue* with sleek nailhead trim. "Each hotel must have an individual character, so I never use assembly-line replicas. Custom designs assure character, ideal silhouettes and scale, and the possibility of eccentricity and experimentation," said Wearstler.

BILLY IDOL *Right* Kelly Wearstler probably did not spend her evenings watching Billy Haines' movies. She's too busy dreaming up new design schemes. Haines made a move from the big screen to the world of decorating, and the chairs in this Viceroy suite are Wearstler's homage to Haines. That's the Pacific Ocean outside. It's real, not a painted backdrop.

with the Avalon and Maison 140 hotels in Beverly Hills and the Viceroy hotel in Palm Springs. "In Los Angeles, where it's often hot, white cools everything down."

Design development for the hotel took about ten months.

"I looked for furniture that was generous and substantial, and chairs that are going to wear well—as well as look glamorous," said Wearstler. "People come to a boutique hotel and expect larger-than-life style. Here the bar stools are white patent leather, and I designed a series of quirky chairs like the Caspar wing chair, and the Midnight Lace ladder-back chair for the Whist bar and the public rooms of Viceroy."

Wearstler designs almost every fabric, wallpaper, accessories and piece of furniture for her hotel and residential projects.

"I seldom find the scale, color, yardage, or silhouette I need to create my vision," she said. One reason her designs look singular and dramatic is that Wearstler has commissioned everything in a room—down to the drawer pulls, an embroidered crest detail on the back of a chair, a cocktail table, wall panels, ceramic whippets, or a reflective wallpaper.

"I embellished and embroidered—and in some cases simplified—the original concepts for the Viceroy," said Wearstler. "Hotel design is a process involving many talented people, many practical considerations. Texture and color and contrast provide surprises, often subliminal. I wanted to make the Viceroy larger than life. For guests, they are stepping out of their every-day lives and entering, in effect, a fantasy, a stage set that really works."

CODE RED

ON A TREE-LINED STREET IN BEVERLY HILLS, KELLY WEARSTLER SCULPTS A HOTEL WITH WIT, NOSTALGIC CHARM, AND BRAVE NEW COLOR

Interior designer Kelly Wearstler could not be accused of having a timorous approach to color. Wearstler studied at the Massachusetts College of Art in Boston and at the School of Visual Arts in New York, and credits her early apprenticeship at the New York design firm, Milton Glaser, Inc., with giving her confidence to design colorful, graphic rooms.

With artful blocks of color and witty design motifs, Wearstler has transformed a mild-mannered thirties Georgian building in Beverly Hills into a chic French embrace of a hotel that mixes Left Bank Paris with twenties Hollywood chinoiserie and cool seventies modernism.

RED ALERT *Left, and opposite* "I didn't want these rooms to be just another banal hotel," said designer Kelly Wearstler, who dreams up everything in her clients' hotels, including the music, the uniforms, the garden style, table décor, and note-paper. "In smaller rooms, I use bold colors and pattern to make the walls disappear, and to give the rooms a feeling of importance," said Wearstler. "I used molding to create the headboards and to give the beds a feel-ing of romance and joy."

"When a client gives me their hotel program, I take it to another level," said Wearstler. "I would get so bored doing typical hotel fare. For me, designing a hotel is like making a movie. I want to transport people to another place, another time. I want guests to feel inspired."

Wearstler and her hotel client traveled in the capitals of Europe and looked at a series of sexy smaller hotels before they planned Maison 140.

"I planned to give a sense of drama and intimacy to the public spaces and the rooms of Maison 140," said the designer. "It's happy décor, with a sense of mystery."

Color is key to Wearstler's brave and bold world. The Bar Noir, a favorite gathering place for in-the-know film and design types, wraps guests in a dark chocolate brown setting, with red and white for contrast.

The lobby of Maison 140 semaphores the bright colors to come in the interiors with an opulent and artful layering of textures and colors. A checkered red-on-red carpet that's very geometrical and very David Hicks, and persimmon wallpaper, underscore red chairs with white woodwork and embroidered pillows. Rich moiré wallpapers add their exotic chinoiserie motif.

Guests linger in the evening at Bar Noir, sipping on the hotel's signature cocktail, the French Kiss, a frisky combination of Champagne and Corvoisier, with a dash of lemon and sugar.

VA-VA VOOM *Left, and below*
Kelly Wearstler would be the
first to say that the suites at
Maison 140 about seduction
and more seduction. Red, the
color of doge's robes and
toile de Jouy patterns that
would have done Marie-
Antoinette proud, meet
embroideries and pristine
white in a mix that's irre-
sistible. The point for
Wearstler is sexy eccentricity
and glamour. Guests applaud
her modern sense of luxe and
sweet dreams, in color, are
assured.

For shopping, there is nearby Barney's of New York and
Neiman Marcus and Maxfield, for the best shoes and fashions in
world. There's people watching on Rodeo Drive and Sunset Plaza,
and a fast book search at Book Soup on Sunset Boulevard.

And when it's time to go out for the evening, Mr. Chow,
Morton's, Spago and Bastide restaurants are just a quick limo
ride away.

It looks like a long stay at Maison 140 is in the stars.

ACKNOWLEDGMENTS

Bouquets and magnums of champagne go to Charles Miers, Klaus Kirschbaum, Gloria Ahn, Jacquie Byrnes, Eva Prinz and Caitlin Leffel at Rizzoli International Publications, and to the amazing team at Subtitle.

Hollywood Houses was first planned on a delirious, inspiring spring visit when Charles, Eva and I drove to design high points around Los Angeles to meet designers and photographers. We began with lunch at Dawnridge, then we dashed into Maxfield (hello, Elton, Diana and Elvis), swept through Therien & Co and Rose Tarlow's Melrose House and stopped at the Chateau Marmont. We were inspired by Hollyhock, Tim Clarke, Book Soup, Indigo Seas, Kelly Wearstler's hotels, Michael Smith's studio, Tim Street-Porter's villa, and bookstores and design stores on La Brea, 3rd, North Robertson, and Beverly. We feasted on the creative spice and fizz of Los Angeles.

Special thanks to our talented designers and architects (and their clients), and to our impressive cast of photographers. Your work shines on these pages, and I am most grateful.

I loved the stories of each interior, the epiphanies of every house hunt, and tales of renovation and the search for beauty, grace, and harmony, reflected on each page. Los Angeles photographers, designers and architects revere and treasure the history and design traditions of the city. Their devotion to invention, reinvention, restoration, and creativity are evident in all the rooms presented here.

DIANE DORRANS SAEKS

PHOTOGRAPHY CREDITS

TIM STREET PORTER
JACKET (FRONT)
INTRODUCTION
CHAPTER 1
Sunlight and Shadow
Dreaming in Technicolor
Pragmatist and Dreamer
CHAPTER 2
Super Schindler
CHAPTER 3
Solace of Beauty
Postcard from Italy
Bella Italia
Superbly Scripted
CHAPTER 4
Room at the Top
Polished to Perfection
An Englishman in Los Angeles
Pasadena Perspective
CHAPTER 5
Chateau Cool

JOHN ELLIS
CHAPTER 1
Screen Gems

DOMINQUE VORILLION
JACKET (BACK)
CHAPTER 2
Plein-Air in Bel-Air
CHAPTER 4
Malibu Luau
The White House
Sleeping Beauty

ART GRAY
CHAPTER 2
For the Love Neutra
Art for Art's Sake
CHAPTER 3
Stairway to Heaven
CHAPTER 4
Hollywood Glory Days

GREY CRAWFORD
CHAPTER 3
A Woman of Style
Pursuit of Happiness
Hotel Glamour Revival
Code Red

JONN COOLIDGE
CHAPTER 4
Island of Calm

MICHAEL MUNDY
CHAPTER 4
Soft Gleam of Gold

JEREMY SAM
CHAPTER 4
A Spirit of Optimism

Ellegance Perfected
Courtesy of the Hotel Bel-Air